Johnny Carson, Ted Williams & Me

The Effect of Three Mother's Toxic Breast Milk on Their Three Sons

R.G. Coleman, Ph.D.

Books by R.G. Coleman, Ph.D.

Is Your Prescription Killing You?

The Governor's Fingerprints

A Mom's Perfect Murder?

The People v. George "Dubya" Bush

God For Smart and Funny People Only

*Trump's Troops Revolt Against
Republican Party's Betrayal*

*Good Dad – Bad Mom – The State's
Criminalization of a Father's Paternal Instincts
Part One*

*Good Dad – Bad Mom – The State's
Criminalization of a Father's Paternal Instincts
Part Two*

Justice for Baby Josh

*Why and How We, the People, Must Remove
Trump*

Books by R;G. Coleman as
Jocelyn Otis-Coleman

My One-Night Stand with God's Assassin

My Daughter's Keeper

In memory of Ted—my dad by proxy, to Henry Bushkin, John Underwood, and Leigh Montville, who provided the primary sources on which the thesis depends, Amber, Patricia (wife #1), who deserved much better, my sister Carol, who rode the train with me part of the way, in memory of my brother Douglas, who paid for his train ticket with his life, and Grady, whose 40 years of friendship has been my beacon..

Premise & Promise

It must be written somewhere that one's greatest strength becomes one's greatest weakness – whether it be civilizations, cultures, countries, governments, institutions, organization, and religions.

This book limits itself to individuals, and more specifically to three sons whose mothers were both the impetus for their heroic rise to fame and fortune, albeit the cause of their inevitable and precipitous fall.

For example, Johnny Carson hated his mother, who he described as a "witch," yet his fame and fortune as America's Number One entertainer was rooted in his childhood need to win his mother's love, affection. and approval by doing magic trick for her through his siblings and neighbors

Ted Williams' Salvation Army mother, was too busy saving souls of the denizens of the "mean streets" of San Diego and Tijuana, to mother Ted, so, Ted, like Johnny, first sought love and affection from those frequenting his neighborhood playground by doing "magic" with his baseball bat on the way to becoming the "greatest hitter who ever lived."

"Me," the most unmothered of the three of us -- my mother abandoned me on the doorstep of a Boston foster home when I was four, was the least successful, and therefore fell the shortest distance.

That Johnny and Ted achieved so much despite their loveless mothers doth make heroes of both, while at the same time providing expert testimony to the simple inexorable truth that a mother's love prevails *uber alles*.)

Johnny Carson: America's Court Jester – America's *Pagliacci*

Johnny Carson was born October 23, 1925, in Corning, Iowa, to Homer Carson, a power company manager, and Ruth Carson, as the middle child to an older sister Catherine and a younger brother Dick. The Carsons lived in southwest Iowa before moving to Norfolk, Nebraska when Johnny was eight.

For reasons more subtle than "middle child syndrome," Johnny felt the need to get his parents approval, especially from his impossible to please mother -- she wore both apron and the "pants."

Johnny's mother may have emotionally abused Johnny – made him the family scapegoat – to assert her authority over the rest of the family-- "Mess with "Mommy Dearest" and I'll do unto you as I do unto Johnny."

By age 12, Johnny is getting attention and approval by doing magic shows for siblings and neighbors, and by age 14, Johnny is earning $3 per performance at local events in Norfolk, Nebraska and later at the University of Nebraska, where he graduated in 1949, with a degree in radio and speech.

His first radio and television job is in Omaha, where he hosts a morning TV program called *The Squirrel's Nest,* in which Johnny interviews courthouse pigeons, as to the political corruption they observe in the courthouse below. He next moves to a CBS affiliate television station in Los Angeles, doing a low-budget *Carson's Cellar,* (1952-1953), and joining the *Red Skelton Show* as a writer, (1954). Skelton "accidently knocks himself unconscious during a show, allowing" Johnny to step in.

In 1955, Jack Benny invites Johnny to appear on his program. Johnny then hosts the game show *Earn*

Your Vacation, and the prime time *The Johnny Carson Show*, which flops.. He's a "regular panelist on *To Tell the Truth*, moves to New York to host *Who Do You Trust?* -- the first show where Johnny adlibs and interviews guests." That show becomes "the hottest item on daytime television." NBC invites Johnny to take over the *Tonight* show, replacing Jack Paar in 1962, which soon becomes *The Tonight Show Starring Johnny Carson*.

Johnny Carson hires Attorney Henry Bushkin in 1970, and over the next nearly 20 years, Johnny Carson and Henry Bushkin are hitched at the hip.

No one, including Johnny's wives – especially Johnny's four wives -- spends more time with Johnny Carson. Henry Bushkin is Johnny's best friend, his almost daily tennis partner, attorney, business partner, unlicensed shrink, surrogate brother, travel companion, referee, marriage counselor, his reluctant partner in crime – breaking into Joanna's (wife #3) apartment looking for evidence of her affair, and Johnny's conscience – his "Jiminy Cricket."

Bushkin KNOWS Johnny Carson. For that reason Johnny Carson 1970 -2005, is excerpted and quoted exclusively from *Johnny Carson*, Henry Bushkin, Houghton Mifflin Harcourt, 2013.

Here's Johnny!!

Anticipating the question, "What is Johnny Carson really like?" Bushkin writes, "…he was endlessly witty and enormously fun to be around …he could also be the nastiest son of a bitch on earth…He was an incredibly complex man, one moment gracious, funny , yet curt, aloof, and hard-hearted in the next…Never have I met a man with less aptitude for, or interest in, maintaining real relationships…But to understand Johnny's complexity, one must first understand his artistry and the esteem in which he was held." (Bushkin p2) (The same artistry and esteem was said of Ted Williams.)

As in the case of Ted Williams, this section about Johnny narrowly asks the question: What is the effect of Johnny Carson's mother, whose death elicited Johnny's response, "The wicked witch is dead," on Johnny's relationships with women, his children, friends, associates, his personality, and his profession?

While at his peak Johnny Carson commanded a nightly adulating audience of 15 million viewers, double the viewers of Leno and Letterman combined, yet he never won the love and approval that he longed for from his mom, who cruelly discredited Johnny as being a second rate son, who try as he would for 79 years, never did please her.

Mommy Dearest of a Different Kind

"PARADISE VALLEY, ARIZ. — Ruth E. Carson, 84, mother of The Tonight Show host Johnny Carson, died Friday at her home after an extended illness."

Johnny's response: "The wicked witch is dead!"…There was no goddamn way to please that woman. She's Macbeth. My marriages failed because she fucked me up" (Bushkin,p.37.

"If a doctor opened up my chest right now, he couldn't find a heart or any goddamn thing. Just a lot of misery. My mother made sure of that. She deprived us all of any goddamn warmth." (Bp 38)

For Johnny, his mother having commandeered the unitary role as "Parent," rendered her opinions, *ex cathedra*, her biases decrees, and her definition of Johnny, gospel – there was no flip side, no buffer, no "good side" of the boy named Johnny Carson. His scapegoat, "untouchable," family status marked him as indelibly as the Star of David on the forehead of a ghetto Jew on Poland in the 1930's.

His mother had effectually castrated his father's soul, if not his body, begging the question: Had. Mr. Carson voluntarily deferred, been forced to abdicate, or was he the victim of a coup, the result being a feckless father, "lame duck," or defrocked dad?

Certainly NOT someone who could, or would, protect, defend, or represent Johnny's interest against the "witch." One can imagine Johnny, as a young boy asking his father permission to go out and play with other neighborhood kids, being advised, "Go ask your mother," who was programmed to say, "No," to Johnny, independent of the question being asked.

Freud instructs us that our personalities are formed by age 6. So what may Johnny have concluded by age 6? 'My mother doesn't' like me and I don't know why…My mother says I'm less important than my sister and brother. I don't know why. I'm afraid of my mother – like she wants to hurt me every chance she gets by what she says, I can't, and don't, trust her. (women) My own mother is my enemy – out to hurt me—make me feel bad about myself. My mother controls everything and everyone. She makes up the rules and is a cruel cop – she twists things I say so she can punish me …If my dad doesn't dare stand up against her, what chance do I have? No chance. No matter what I do to get her to love me – to stop hating me –she still hates me, but I'm too scared, so I have to keep trying…'

(On a personal note, one of my first jobs after undergraduate college was working with incarcerated male juveniles, ages 12-16, most all of whom came from inner-city ghettos in eastern Massachusetts, and whose file showed mom to be a drug addict and/or a prostitute, and certainly the mother of many children with many fathers. Yet, two words: "You're mother," would spur the prison runt – the receiver of this "unkindest cut of all" into a no-holds- barred attack on the prison bully who dared utter such a pejorative.)

Moms, including Ruth Carson, despite incontrovertible evidence of cruelty, depravity, and mischievous mothering, are granted immunity from prosecution by their sons, to wit, Johnny Carson could not utter the words, "I hate my mother," even from a distance.

When asked about Johnny's relationship with his father, Johnny, noted, "Everybody likes Dad, but he lets her walk all over him. Every once in a while dad lets out a peep, and it's the Soviet Union and Czechoslovakia – she just rolls out the tanks." (Bp88)

Johnny once sent his parents around the world on a cruise to mark one of their wedding anniversaries. It was a forty-seven day trip, with all accommodations entirely first class. Johnny even gave them an American Express card to cover anything they wanted to buy …Johnny never hears from them during the trip..

Bushkin recalls that Johnny knows exactly when his parent would be arriving back in Scottsdale – the home Johnny bought for them, after Johnny's mother returned the fur coat Johnny purchased for her, telling Johnny she'd rather have a home where it was so warm, no one wore fur coats. But days go by and still no call from his parents as to how, or if, they enjoyed the trip.

Finally, Johnny calls. His dad answers "How was the trip?" Johnny asks.

"Hold on, son, "I'll get your mother on the line.""

All she says when she picks up the phone. is "Well, son. We are so happy to be home."

As before, Johnny laughs at his mother'

rudeness, but he didn't really find it funny. (Bp89-90) (America's *Pagliacci* – laughing on the outside crying inside.)

So it was for 30 years, Johnny Carson, America's court (TV) jester, host of *The Tonight Show Starring Johnny Carson* -- darling of 15 million sleepless Americans, joking and causing them to laugh away that day's *Sturm und Drang.*

On stage, always smiling and laughing, often at himself – a task enabled by "mommy dearest,' Johnny was the little boy/man with a mischievous twinkle in his eyes revealing he knew he was gaming his audience, seeking the recognition, love, and affection from the 15 million TV viewers denied him by his mother.

> *"All the World's a stage,*
> *And all the men and women merely players*
> *They have their exits and their entrances,*
> *And one man in his time plays many parts.*
> Shakespeare - *As You Like It*

Johnny played his part of a son mortally wounded by the outrageous misfortune of being birthed by the unkindest kind of mother, with extraordinary skill, artistry, and heroism.

Yet, Johnny's problems remained undisturbed by his performance on stage. First, "Tonight's" opioid effect lasted only 60 -- 90 minutes – not nearly long enough to mitigate Johnny's years of pain caused by his mother. Second, Johnny was left with 22.5 to 24 hours each day, plus weekends, holidays, and vacations to live absent his opiate – alcohol helped, but frequently exacerbated Johnny's bad mothering problem.

Johnny left his mother's funeral arrangements to his sister Catherine, and did not attend the funeral. He didn't attend his father's funeral either, reasoning, "The only time I want to go to a funeral is when I want to make sure the son of a bitch is really dead," (Bp244), which would seem to have been ample reason to be in the front row of Ruth Carson's funeral.

Truman Capote, saw Johnny frequently as tenants in the UN Plaza, opined, "I met his mother once. "She was an absolute bitch. Despite everything he's done, she's never really accepted him, and he constantly seeks her approval. That's what keeps him going …In my opinion, Ruth Carson soured her son to the point where it was damn near impossible for him to be happy with any woman for any extended period of time, with people in general," (Bp 245)

Johnny's Wives: No Henry VIII Here

In 1949, Johnny married Jody Wolcott, his college sweetheart, and mother to his only children, sons Christopher, Richard ("Rick"), and Cory.

In 1959, Jody and Johnny separate, and in 1963, Jody obtains a Mexican divorce.. Under the terms Johnny pays Jody $15,000 in alimony and "7,500 in child support. Jody explains, "We had three children right away and there was no money. It happens all the time to a lot of people.

Johnny described that marriage as his greatest personal failure." (Bp65)

Later that same year, Johnny marries Joanne Copeland. Seven years later, Johnny, discovers that Joanne has surreptitiously leased a separate apartment in which she is "pleasuring" former New York Giants football star Frank Gifford.

Johnny laments, ""I'm not surprised that Joanne did this to me, but it hurts like hell. Maybe I drove her to it. I wasn't the best husband in the world. I should have been home more. Not out running around …I'm a shit. I have three children with my first wife and I don't see any of them." (Bp36)

They divorce in 1972 (9 years). Next, Johnny marries Joanna Holland, a 31 year-old model, but not before doing a background check.– She passes, but Johnny fails – again. Despite the appearance of the "good life" – travel to the Riviera and London, winning the Hasty Pudding Man of the Year Award from Harvard, Johnny's infidelities lead inexorably to increasingly frequent skirmishes, Johnny moves into the Beverly Hills Hotel – It is rumored Johnny has acquired Beverly Hills Hotel as a home away from home, followed by Johnny re-establishing squatters rights in bed beside Joanna contingent upon lavish gifts of jewelry and a white Rolls Royce Corniche.

After only two years, they separate, leaving behind a third trail of Johnny's egregious mistreatment, negligence, and dereliction of husbandry.

It appears that Johnny is consumed with two competing compulsions – The compulsion to prove he can please a woman despite a lifetime of being unable to please his mother, versus his compulsion to displace his anger toward his mother onto women in general, and his wives in particular.

He can't love women, or anyone, because he has never been loved. No precedent has been established for love, as it would be in a "normal relationship between mother and son. He can use his money and fame to "buy" any female he wants, but as soon as she ascertains she's been bought, she wants out, and/or she discovers Johnny is "cheating," she cheats back, and eventually decides, well if Johnny thought he's bought me, I'll make him pay dearly for my freedom from him. Then the cycle begins anew, *ad infinitum.* .

Meanwhile, Johnny says things, and commits acts he knows will drive her away, or into the arms/loins of another, but, because he is compelled to make each current wife pay for the past sins of his cruel and abusive mother, he cannot do otherwise.

Expensive gifts to her may temporarily relieve his guilt, but over time she concludes the gifts are more for Johnny than for her.

For his part, Johnny believes he shouldn't be expected to consider the emotional needs and wants of his wives and lovers as neither of his parents considered his needs and wants. All relationships are eventually doomed if he continues to ignore their emotional needs and wants, yet only by mistreating them does he relieve himself of the festering hate of his mother.

Then, too, if she cheats, Johnny's lamentations brew in the distillery of his own bitterness –'They're all witches like my mother.'

In short, Johnny has unwittingly wandered into a lose/lose situation.

Joanna and Johnny divorce in 1985. (13 years).

Johnny reflects""My giving advice on marriage is like the captain of the *Titanic* giving lessons on navigation." (Bp216)

That same year, Johnny begins dating Alexis "Alex" Maas, a blond in her early 30's, Hollywood-attractive, who once worked for Governor Dukakis and presidential candidate from Massachusetts.

Johnny married Joanne the same year he divorced Jody, married Joanna the same year he divorced Joanne, and married Alex the same year he divorced Joanna. And while each divorce may have been provoked by Johnny's affair with his next wife, the compulsive pattern of his marriages begs the following questions: Was Johnny obsessed with being married? If so, wouldn't he be more disciplined in his husbandry?

To the contrary, he was as carelessly compulsive in his affairs as he was as being a husband.

Was he determined to prove his mother wrong by acquiring someone to love him – make Johnny feel he was Number One? If so, that scheme was similarly doomed as Johnny had no experience with being loved – feeling Number One, nor would he have known how to maintain and sustain a loving relationship.

It seems more likely that Johnny's compulsion to be married and have affairs – always have a woman present – was to deal with his toxic relationship with his mother by replaying the "love to hatred turned," with each and every woman to which Johnny attached himself.

Each marriage had a beginning – adolescent sexual attraction – Johnny's ego-feeding trophy, a middle – mistreated wife and multiple affairs -- displaced anger toward his mother – make her hurt as he perceives his mother hurt him, and an end -- "love to hatred turned".

Johnny's wealth and fame allowed him to over-indulge himself in his mini-dramas – make so many woman pay for his mother's sins. But just as it was with each and every winless war against his mother, Johnny lost these proxy wars too – twofold – Rejection all over again and millions in alimony and support.

.Johnny orders a background check on Alexis as he had done on Joanna. Alexis' is remarkable for being so unremarkable.

Two years after they met, they marry at Johnny's home a t Malibu, on June 20, 1987. Johnny's brother Dick is the only guest other than the officiating Judge.

A speaker -phone offers play-by-play to Alex's parents in Pittsburg. The honeymoon is a honeymoon of convenience – Johnny's convenience, of course: They attend Wimbledon in London, which Johnny does annually anyway.

On the cruise of the Italian Riviera which

follows Wimbledon, while dining one evening on the yacht, Alex says something "so inconsequential," but Johnny, already in a bad mood for no apparent reason, looked her straight in the eye and said, "We've been married for three weeks. If you say something like that again, this marriage won't last another three weeks." (Bp 253

The relationship between Carson and Bushkin ended bitterly in 1988, as had all of Carson's relationships – "from love to hatred turned," so Buskin knew little as to Johnny's marriage to Alex.

The consensus is that they lived in Malibu, traveled, and that their 18 years together were relatively uneventful.

Only Alex, tolerated bad Johnny's verbal abuse. Only Alex was there until the end

Children Sacrificed on the Altar of Their Famous Father's Fame

Johnny and his first wife, Jody had three sons Christopher, Richard ("Rick") and Cory Carson,

That so little is known of Johnny's relationship with his three sons may be excused as Johnny's attempt to shield his family from public scrutiny. That flawed reasoning fails when exposed in the glaring lights of the media coverage of his wives and other business and professional relationships..

The exception to the rule is Johnny's middle son – Rick, who like Johnny, joined the navy. At age 20, while Rick is stationed in a remote Alaskan outpost, he began "drinking heavily and exhibiting suicidal tendencies," ultimately landing him in the military Psychiatric ward of New York City's Bellevue Hospital, an incident which seems to have reminded Johnny of his dereliction of duty as a father -- Johnny never visited, Rick, but instead turned the matter over to Bushkin.

In 1985, Johnny asks that Rick be given a job "somewhere" in Carson Productions. Rick is hired as stage manager in the production of *Amen*, a key position and if it's not being performed well, the entire production notices.

Rick is habitually late, drinks on the job, and is subsequently fired. Johnny blames Rick's boss and threatens to fire him.

October 1987, at the 25th Anniversary party of the Tonight Show on the *Queen Mary*, Rick is again drinking heavily. Johnny goes to Rick to save father and son further embarrassment, but instead throws gasoline on the fire – father and son are soon venting past enmities – Before Johnny's raised fist strikes Rick, Bushkin and others pull Johnny away. (Bp 262-263)

On June 21, 1991, Rick is killed when the car he is driving plunges off a steep embankment. On the following Tonight Show, Johnny shares some of Rick's photos with the audience, before the curtain of silence falls again on Johnny's three sons.

Personality: Public Happy Face – Private Mad/Sad Face

Bushkin wrote, "But on that night in 1979 ....I finally experienced a moment in which I recognized his true stature" ...a party at the palatial home of Ginny and Henry Mancini of *Moon River, Breakfast at Tiffany's* and *Days of Wine and Roses* fame ...20 Grammy's and three Oscars, celebrating but another of Mancini's many awards.

Among the guests are Jack Lemmon, Jane Fonda, Walter Matthau, Gene Kelly, Sean Connery,

Michael Caine, Jimmy Stewart, Cary Grant, Tony Curtis, Andre Previn – all asking Bushkin some form of the question, "Where's Johnny?"

"…nearly all had been on the *Tonight Show,* but none of them knew Johnny well. It struck me that most of them genuinely wanted him to come, were genuinely interested in meeting him, curious to see him up close, and hoping to get to know him better. You could see how Johnny's general aloofness from the Hollywood scene actually drew people to him-- how his relative unavailability on the social circuit restored the mystique that his nightly presence on the tube corroded … despite their enormous talents, none of these actors could do what Johnny did …They played characters -- inhabited invented identities, brought to life a carefully constructed script. But Johnny took the stage just as himself, reliant on his own native gifts. Night after night he performed live to tape in a medium that permitted no rewrites …no retakes …when they appeared on the *Tonight Show,* Johnny helped them by drawing out the qualities that made them seem interesting, glamorous, witty, and fun, frequently using self-deprecation – the straight-man to their jokester – the fan to their stardom…And on that night at the Mancinis' after hearing the eagerness and even tension in the voices of Hollywood's greatest luminaries, asking me, "Where's Johnny?," I saw the singular respect he'd earned among his peers. He is indeed a star among stars." …At long last, the Carsons arrive. They pull up in the white Rolls-Royce Corniche that Johnny had given Joanna earlier that year, reparation for some earlier indiscretion…He smiling, she hugging, they offer neither excuses nor explanations. It didn't matter." (Bp2-10)

There was a Dr. Jekyll and Mr. Hyde -- good Johnny and bad Johnny swing to Johnny's personality.

Good Johnny -- uncommonly generous – sending his parents on an all expense paid around the world, to bad Johnny announcing, "The wicked witch is dead," upon learning of his mother's death.

As Johnny avoided parties, formal, or informal, as a young child avoids the dentist's chair. Bushkin describes those parties which Johnny could not avoid as constituting real work for him -- as "torture."" (Bp 13). (Ted Williams did Johnny one better; he refused all social occasions requiring a tie, and most others, even when he was the guest of honor.. If it is true that confidence comes only from a mother's love – how could it be otherwise – a son would feel worthy if his own mother didn't value him?)

And of course, never having been praised by his mother, he would simultaneously seek praise from others – 15 million TV viewers of *The Late Show Starring Johnny Carson,* yet be suspicious of those praising him in person. No matter what he did, it failed to win his mother's love and appreciation, so why would anyone else, particularly strangers, pay Johnny tribute, unless, of course, they were trying get something in return, from Johnny?

"Bad Johnny" was suspicious, hostile, and abusive. The solution? Control -- Be Number One in the eyes of 15 million TV viewers each night, safely tucked in their beds where they can neither hurt, reject, or get close to, Johnny – make personal emotional reciprocity demands on Johnny he did not know how to fulfill, and couldn't and wouldn't fulfill anyway.

As a little boy, he couldn't prevent his mother's emotional abuse by distancing himself from his mother – as an adult, television provided Johnny that distance – safe harbor. Similarly, in his multiple sexual partners and four wives, the intimacy of the sex act allowed Johnny physical closeness without a commensurate emotional commitment – as if Johnny was a paying gigolo.

It worked for Johnny, aided and abetted by his fame and fortune, which was also the glue that held the relationship together, whether for one-night, the length of the affair, or the time of the marriage. It worked for his wives only as long as his extravagant life style, and being billed as "Johnny's wife," trumped his insouciance, his infidelities, and his inevitable displaced rage toward his mother made victim of his wives.

As with most males, Johnny's ethics had the same integrity as a Jimmy Swaggart sermon on infidelity, to wit, Johnny could fuck who would let him – there is no record of those , if any, who refused, while if his wives' or lovers' violated the law of monogamy – one mate at a time – off with their heads – maidenheads never being an issue,

So it was that when Johnny found out that Joanne had rented an apartment which she was sharing with a male other than Johnny, that Johnny, with a loaded revolver, broke into her apartment, found evidence that Joanne's lover was ex-New York Giants football great Frank Gifford, that Johnny " leans against her living room wall and begins to weep." (Bp32-33), never asking how often his infidelities had caused Joanne to weep, or if his infidelities had caused her to rent the apartment and take Frank Gifford as her love

Johnny's vices – addictions— in addition to sex, are alcohol and cigarettes. His sex addiction could have gotten him shot, but instead just cost him millions in divorces, his alcohol addiction might have killed him later-- cirrhosis of the liver, if his addiction t nicotine hadn't killed him first– respiratory failure due to emphysema.

Bushkin writes, "Drinking was always an adventure with Johnny; two drinks were enough to place him into a twilight zone from which he could appear hostile, nasty, "bad Johnny," or a very funny "good Johnny."

Johnny says he started smoking in 1939; at age 14, asserts he can't quit, doesn't want to quit and doesn't want anyone telling him he should quit. (Bp29) (A declaration of suicide he fulfilled on January 23, 2005, at age 79.)

Having been relegated to being disfavored in his family of five – adult Johnny insists that in all marriages, social relationships, professional and business dealings, he be automatically installed as Number One – no exceptions. In marriages, that meant Johnny's wives must be glamorous – pay tribute to Johnny's sexuality and tenuous prowess – play the role of Johnny's trophy, accept his entitlement to unlimited sexual partners, while demanding his wives' monogamy.

Having abdicated his role as father to his three sons, rather that attempt to be Number One in their eyes, he simply retreated from that battlefield, his sword never unsheathed..

Social relationships were not so easily manipulated. First, Johnny, for reasons already cited, lacked the ego strength, confidence, and bravado to upstage the likes of Sinatra, Jimmy Stewart, or Cary Grant, Second, Johnny had neither the social or political skills to match Bob Hope or Bing Crosby. Third, Johnny was a stripper in a glass cage – look, listen, but don't touch – don't get close to. For Johnny that glass cage was the TV screen. Fourth, Johnny didn't trust people – expected they would take advantage of him as his mother had done. Johnny was essentially a loner, who for 90-60 minutes, would perform – be America's contemporary court jester, and then, as soon as his curtain fell, would revert to his very private world of friendless self-indulgence.

In his book, Bushkin offers two examples of Johnny's striving for Number One.

Johnny had accepted the offer to host President Reagan's inaugural extravaganza. Before the event began, Buskin noted that Bob Hope presented some papers to Johnny saying, "I've written some lines you might like to use," to which Johnny quipped, "Can you imagine the nerve of the man to think that I needed jokes from him?"(Bp168)

Next, " In tears, Johnny's wife Joanna complains to Johnny that Ed McMahon's wife had better seats than she did."

The director of the broadcast of the inauguration promises Johnny he will not change nor alter Johnny's monologue, but does so anyway, thereby compounding Johnny's feeling of being less than Number One.

Johnny believes he will be getting a VP tour of the White House, when in fact, it is the same guided tour offered the general public/.

Johnny has not only had his Number One status shredded, but he is now a member of the "petty pace," no more special than the ten other people in the tour.

Johnny's fall from grace must have been duly noted by person or persons close to Reagan, because, the President of the United States calls to apologize and to invite the Carson's to dinner the next time the President and Nancy are back in Los Angeles.

"Carson's ego had grown so large that only a call from the President could pacify him."(Bp170-174)

(After all those years of his mother treating Johnny as *unter Mensch,* he now demands to be treated as *uber Mensch.*

Another time, Johnny is to host the grand opening of Caesars Palace, and is told he can bring as many guests as he wants, Caesars Palace will not only pick up the tab, but his guests will get a refund of the plane ticket in casino chips. Johnny invites 350 including his parents,

When Johnny arrives to check in as the Number One Vegas, attraction making his debut as host of the town's premier hotel, the clerk tells Johnny his suite won't be ready for 30 minutes, " Johnny goes ballistic, orders Bushkin to "charter a plane back to Los Angeles, c announcing, I won't work here!"

All attempts to appease Number One fail, including reminding Johnny that his parents his other 348 guest are on their way, to which Johnny snaps, "I don't give a shit! I won't spend one minute more with this monumental incompetents!"

Only the offer by Caesar's Palace main man's personal apartment – 10,000 square feet of rooftop opulence – swimming pool, Jacuzzi, wine cellar, health spa, six bedrooms, and a living room to accommodate 300 people, placates Johnny's pique.

"Every time you come to Caesar's. This is where you will stay."

"Nice, says Johnny, but I don't see a tennis court up here."

"No, it's downstairs." (The head pro is the then internationally famous Pancho Gonzales)." Any time you want to hit with him, it's on me …I've never let anyone stay up here, not even Sinatra. But, I owe this to you as a show of my appreciation for your working here."

The weekend is saved." (Bp 192-194).

(Déjà vu. First, the President of the United States, Ronald Reagan and now the main man at Caesars Palace indulge Johnny in his fantasy that despite his mother's placing Johnny last, President Reagan, and the main man at Caesar's Palace anoint him Number One.)

Bushkin writes, "Nowhere is the change in

Johnny's personality more evident than on the tennis court… He is always capable of indulging his petulant, sore loser side, but during this period, his language becomes nastier, his anger more demonstrative, and his line calls more bold. Longtime tennis buddies now frequently find that their schedules are full, including baseball Hall of Famer Hank Greenberg, who tires of Johnny's curses and self-serving line calls. No one wants to play tennis with Johnny anymore. He subsequently resigns his membership. (Bp 223-234)

Johnny's mother dies in 1989, Upon learning of her death, Johnny snarls, "The wicked witch is dead, relegates the funeral arrangements to his older sister, and refuses to attend his mother's funeral, as testimony to the accumulated hurt Johnny perceives he suffered from his mother's toxic mothering.

"Johnny Carson enjoyed the adulation of millions, yet his mother denied him a mother's love and seemed to enjoy making certain he knew. He carried that pain, and spread it, all his life." (Bp244-247)

As with all Johnny Carson's wives, his sons, his tennis and business associates, Johnny's nearly 20 year personal and professional relationship with his attorney, Henry Bushkin suddenly and inexplicably crashed when Carson falsely accused Bushkin of "cheating," on Carson, saying, "I hear you're trying to steal my goddamn company …Sixty million Where the fuck did that number come from? You and Weinberger got a sweet deal for yourselves? …I've talked to Ed Hookstratten." (One of Beverly Hills's most prestigious attorneys) "He'll take over. Let's talk about you. What's fair between us?"

Bushkin, stunned, offers, "One year's compensation paid over the next 12 months and my share of the proceeds when the company," (Carson Productions) is sold."

"It's a deal."

They shake hands. Bushkin exits. (Bp69)

(After nearly 20 years of being Johnny Carson's lawyer, confidant, best friend, tennis partner, surrogate brother, marriage counselor, business partner, and good will ambassador, Bushkin is suddenly and summarily fired on Carson's suspicion of a conspiracy which existed only in Johnny Carson's mind.)

Johnny's manager, Sonny Werblin, former president of the New York Jets, opined, "Jack Benny was the unhappiest man I have ever known. And Benny is Carson's idol. Johnny is the second –unhappiest person I've ever known." (Bp28.)

On January 24, 2005. at Cedars-Sinai Medical Center, Johnny Carson died of respiratory failure due to emphysema – smoking cigarettes since he was 14. – ALONE - Not a single fan, friend, or relative was at his deathbed

The Effect of Johnny's Mother's Toxic Breast Milk on Johnny

Johnny, Ted and I each had toxic relationships with our mothers, but Johnny's "mother problem" is simple. He hated her. On learning of his mother's death, Johnny noted, "The wicked witch is dead,"

Ted was torn between his love of his mother and the pain he felt from her neglect. Johnny seemed to have no such conflict; he hated his cold, controlling, and cruel mother -- felt betrayed by her.

If his own mother betrayed him, it follows that everyone else would do the same. No one could be trusted. For Johnny, it was never a question if he was going to be betrayed, but, when, and by whom. Sometimes, as in the case of Bushkin, Johnny contrived the betrayal.

Still, he could never stop trying to please his mother. He bought her a mink coat. She returned it. He took her to a lavish Hollywood party attended by Hollywood's super-stars. His mother commented, "Well, I guess parties are all the same." He sent his mother and father on an all-expense paid, 47 day cruise. She never called to let Johnny know how well the cruise was going, nor did she call to thank him when she returned home. Finally Johnny calls her. "It's nice to be home," was her only response,"

It must have seemed to Johnny that his mother was telling him in every cruel way she could, "Don't try to please me – make me love you. I don't, and I never will. Knock yourself out."

But, as a boy, Johnny had already tried extra hard to gain her approval by learning magic, doing shows at local events, leading him to major in radio and speech at the University of Nebraska. He was soon climbing the ladder to a successful career in entertainment. Was he going to abandon all that just because it hadn't succeeded in winning his mother's approval? Not a chance. With a turn of the screw, Johnny set out to prove the "wicked witch" wrong by becoming, the world's Number One TV entertainer" as host of *The Johnny Carson Tonight Show* – "in-her-face " proof his mother was wrong for having assigned Johnny least favored status.

Johnny's Rule: "I have to be Number One," in all matters foreign or domestic – business or marital," (Bp101-102), for two reasons: First, to prove his mother wrong, and second, to demand inexorable loyalty against betrayers.

Both failed of course. His mother was indifferent to his success, and his demand for Number One deference ran amuck among his infidelities and his predisposition to accuse business associates of betraying him without probable cause.

Ted, Johnny and I had weak, feckless fathers, making our relationships with our mothers – sink or swim -- We three sank.

Johnny acknowledged, "Everybody likes Dad, but he lets her walk all over him. Every once in a while dad lets out a peep, and it's the Soviet Union and Czechoslovakia – she just rolls out the tanks." (Bp88)

In a way *The Johnny Carson Show* was a party – a bedroom party, in which Johnny's guests were kept at a safe distance while the host performed his magic on his terms, under his control, and therefore immune to betrayal.

Ted, Johnny, and I, absent the experience of having bonded with our mothers, were nevertheless, compelled – propelled – to try to bond with a woman, unaware that our very inexperience precluded us from gaining a working knowledge of the needs and wants of women. As a result, our wives described us as "impossible to live with," "irascible explosive, short-fused, verbally abusive, foul-mouthed, scape-goating, sometimes cruel, and habitually making the present wife pay for past sins of our mothers.

We three each had four wives – not three, not five, but four wives. Johnny first marries his college sweetheart Jody Wolcott, mother to his only children, Christopher, Richard ("Rick"), and Cory. Ten years later, they separate and in 1963, Jody obtains a divorce. explaining,, "We had three children right away and there was no money." Johnny describes it as his greatest personal failure." (Bp65)

That same year, Johnny marries Joanne Copeland. Seven years later, Johnny, this time correctly suspecting betrayal, breaks -into Joanne's "other" apartment where he finds proof that Joanne's lover is former New York Giants great Frank Gifford. Joanne and Johnny divorce in 1972 (9 years).Johnny marries his third wife, Joanna. They divorce in 1985, (13 years). which to Johnny, was the "unkindest cut of all"

That same year, Johnny begins dating Alexis "Alex" Maas, and marries her two years later. This marriage seems to have lasted as long as Johnny did, although there may have been some separations. Johnny now no longer in the spotlight, interest in his personal life waned concurrently.   .

Johnny's wives may be seen as but the tip of the iceberg – four wives among perhaps a hundred affairs and one-night stands – lays -- each woman unwittingly used by Johnny to extract the " love" he never got from his mother – if not love, then sex as its substitute, a "win" where before he had lost..

.Johnny, unable to bond with his mother, and therefore with any woman, did the next best thing; he copulated with many women, but was unable to give or receive love from not one.

Ted. Johnny, and I, each a victim of bad parenting, became bad dads. Johnny admits being a father to his three sons *in absentia.* The exception being his middle son, Rick – a classic middle child syndrome - - who has a "nervous breakdown"' while in the navy, is hospitalized in the military psychiatric ward of New York's Bellevue Hospital, is fired from the job as stage manager on one of Johnny's production for being drunk on the job, and who, during the 25th fifth anniversary of *The Tonight Show*, gets so out of control Johnny has to ;intervene. An ugly shouting match ensues during which someone has to grab Johnny's arm to keep him from slugging Rick. On June 24, 1991, Rick is killed when his car plunges over a steep embankment.

Ted, Johnny, and I, without the unconditional love of a mother, developed dysfunctional self-destructive personalities, which repulsed the very social belonging we coveted, in turn, guaranteeing us the loneliness and sense of abandonment we so feared.

Johnny Carson retires in 1992. During his 30 years as host of *The Tonight Show Starring Johnny Carson*-- October 1.1962 – May 22, 1992, Johnny Carson wins six Emmys, the Governor's Award, Outstanding Variety Music, or Comedy Program Award, (series), The Peabody Personal Award, American Comedy Funniest Male Performer in a TV Series Award, and in 1992, the Lifetime Achievement Award. Johnny is inducted into the Television Academy Hall of Fame (1987), is awarded the Presidential Medal of Freedom (1992) and a Kennedy Center Honor (1993).

In the end, the consensus of Johnny's Hollywood peers and his millions of fans, is that Johnny Carson is indeed Number One, thereby allowing Johnny to, at long last, experience the love and status his mother denied him – a hero who had triumphed over the greatest loss a son could suffer – he had been denied his mother's love.

A Pyrrhic victory at best, for on January 24, 2005, at Cedars-Sinai Medical Center, Johnny Carson dies of respiratory failure due to emphysema – smoking cigarettes since he was 14, and forbidding any one to try to convince him to stop.

No family, no fans, and no friends – by then he didn't have any-- are at his bedside.

Johnny Carson, beloved by millions of TV viewers, died alone, bitter for having failed for 79 years to secure his mother's love, or its equivalent, from four wives, hundreds of sex partners, a life of profane luxury, and an estate of $ 450 million. Johnny died a broken man – mortally wounded by his toxic mother. The man who made millions laugh every night for over 30 years, yet was described as "the second –unhappiest person I've ever known." – America's Pagliacci!

Ted Williams: Baseball's Mozart --
Baseball's Genius

Summer of 1946. I'm 10. After rushing to wash my hands for supper, I scamper down the stairs (By grabbing the railing on both sides, I catapult to the floor bypassing the last five steps. THUD.

The old console radio under the front living-room window, broadcasts the Red Sox game from Detroit... Top of the ninth. The Sox are losing by one run. Wally Moses singles. Ted steps into the batter's' box. I imagine his bat cocked, his chin over his front shoulder, body torqued like a cobra ready to strike, his eyes fixed on the ball like an bald eagle's on a field mouse -- It's s as if life itself holds its breath.

CRACK! With the speed of light, the sound of Ted's bat travels from Detroit to my living room. I see the ball climbing high into the Detroit sky on its obit out of Briggs Stadium – Ted's two-run home run wins the game!

Once again, Ted Williams, my deity, my surrogate dad - defies the gods of odds.

To Begin Again

In *My Turn at Bat*, as told to John Underwood, Simon & Schuster, NY, 1967,which is the primary source of information as to Ted's life 1918-1960, Ted, the older of two sons describes being raised in a little house on Utah Street in San Diego, His mother had gotten the house through the generosity of a prominent family. Ted believes his mother was supposed to pay them back, but doesn't think she ever did. Ted later valued the house at $4,000.

He recalls being ashamed of how dirty the house was all the time, and particularly when baseball scouts like Eddie Collins, General Manager of the Red Sox, came calling, and had to sit in the chair which had a towel covering the hole revealing the springs

Ted remembers spending most of his time at the North Park Playground, a block and a half from his house. "The Park had lights, so we could play a game called "Big League," until nine o'clock at night. All it took was two guys, a bat and one of those softballs with the high seams to make the ball curve, drop, screwball, and knuckleball."

Ted would get to school so early he would have to wait for the janitor to open the school so he could get the balls and bats ready for the other kids. (I did Ted one better. I rode a school bus. The first day of school, I announced on the bus, "Scrub One for the year," meaning I would be the first batter up before school and during recess for the entire year.)

Ted recalls, at lunch, he would run home and get a sack full of fried potatoes, run all the way back so he could get in fifteen more minutes of ball.

.The North Park Playground where Ted spent more waking hours than he did at home was a block from Ted's house,

The playground Director, Rod Luscomb was described by Ted as being a husky six feet three inches, in his late 30's – early 40's who never got beyond the California State Leaguer, but was Ted's first hero. (surrogate father)

Mr. Cassie, who lived across the street, worked as a high school janitor, and loved to fish, was another father figure for Ted. None of Mr. Cassie's sons liked to fish so he'd take Ted on a weekend fishing trips.. thereby beginning Ted's life-long passion for fishing.

Mr. Cassie gave Ted a fountain pen when Ted

graduated from high school. (Ted received no graduation gift from his father or mother.)

When Mr. Cassis died Ted felt as bad as when his own father died." (Probably worse if the truth were to be admitted).

By the time Ted was working with John Underwood, on :*My Turn at Bat*,", Ted opined, "My dad didn't take much interest in me until I got to the point where baseball contracts were being offered me. Then he liked to be in on the act, but in the real crises of my life, he never once gave me advice."

Ted's brother Danny had bone marrow "Danny once threw an orange at somebody and broke his arm." (Any connection to Ted's history of bone problems – broken elbow, broken collarbone (twice), ankle, and ribs?) Both Danny and Ted's son, John Henry died of leukemia.)

As predicted, a tall skinny, awkward, self-deprecating nail-biting, nervous, teenage Ted Williams, "never went out much with girls …If a girl looked at me twice, I'd run the other way"

Ted lists his high school baseball coach Wes Caldwell at Herbert Hoover High in San Diego, as being the person who first influenced him to become a baseball player. "

"Coach Caldwell tells the story that on the first day of practice, "I hit a couple balls on the cafeteria roof and the janitor came running out and made us change fields.…One day I hit a ball they say went 450 feet. I fell down rounding second, and again rounding third – a big skinny kid, all arms and legs. I got thrown out at home plate."

A scout for the Detroit Tigers watches Ted's last game in high school. He told Ted's mother that Ted was too "scrawny" -- six foot three and 145 pounds -- a year of professional baseball would- literally kill Ted.

Seventeen year-old Ted signs his first contract to play professional baseball with the San Diego Padres in 1936, for $150 a month   (At age 42, Ted's contract is the highest in baseball at $120,000.)   "

That winter (1937) Ted is sold to the Boston Red Sox for a reported $35,000 and two players. That March, Ted is shipped to Red Sox's farm team in Minneapolis

Ted remembers t he afternoon he let two ground balls go through his legs and strikes out twice..

"I'm so damn mad after the second strikeout that when I get to the bench, I keep right on going into the clubhouse -- just disgusted and thinking it was my last at bat anyway. I'm half undressed when the bat boy comes running in yelling at me to get back out there. We've started a big rally. The score is 6-4, two men on, two out, and I'm due up. I'm still fumbling with my buttons on my uniform when I get out there. Wouldn't you know it? I hit the first pitch out of the park and we won, 7-6."

The next year, Ted moves up to the Boston Red Sox. His rookie season he hits a home run in every park completing the list in Yankee stadium on the last day. Babe Ruth declares Ted to be' Rookie of the Year," before there was an official "Rookie of the Year

Ted chose not to home that winter (1939).. "Home was never a happy place for me – my father and mother were never really together. My brother was always in some kind of scrape. While I was trying to help my mother, she's giving everything to my brother. I'm mad at that. I try to give my mother everything she wants, but I could never give her all I really wanted to give her because she would give it to my brother. If it was a refrigerator or a washing machine, he'd hock it. … my mother and father separate and there is more grief, so I stayed away. And you know what a Boston sports writer wrote the first time I did something to displease him? "Well what do you expect from a guy who won't even go see his mother in the off season?'

Ted, nicknamed "The Kid" for his naïve, uncensored, ingenuous, spontaneous, unfiltered, self-made rules of fairness and honesty, became easy prey for the battle-scarred Boston baseball writers guided by one unprincipled principle: Write to sell newspapers – *The Boston Globe, The Boston Herald, The Record/American, and the Christian Science Monitor* – the truth, the facts, and journalistic integrity be damns!

Ted, perhaps a victim of the "sophomore jinks" believes he slipped in 1940, even though his batting average was actually higher at .344 and he lead the league in runs scored. But he only hit 23 home runs, and only seven in Fenway Park.

1940 is also the beginning of the war between Ted and the Boston sports press. That was also the year Ted got booed for making an error and then for striking out. Wounded by the unfairness of the fans, Ted vowed he would never tip his hat to the fickle fans when they applauded, (He never did.)

In the 1941 season, fan interest and tension builds as Ted flirts to becoming the first to hit /400 since Bill Terry hit .401 in 1930. .

Ted is batting .436 in June, down to .402 in late August, and then up again to .413 in September, but down to 39955 -- .400 going into the last game of the season, actually a doubleheader at Philadelphia.

In *My Turn at Bat*, Ted remembers, "The night before the game my manager, Joe Cronin, offers to take me out of the lineup to preserve the .400. I tell Cronin if I couldn't hit .400 all the way I don't deserve it. It sure as hell meant something to me.

. "In Detroit that July I had hit what remains to this day the most thrilling hit of my life… I'm in my second All-Star game. I had a double which drives in a run in the fourth inning, but Arky Vaughan of the Pirates has hit two home runs for the National League and he looked like the hero of the day. We go into the ninth trailing 5-3. There are five men scheduled to bat in front of me and when the first batter pops out I have to think I won't get another chance. Then the next batter gets an infield hit, followed by a single and a base on balls. The bases are loaded .and Joe DiMaggio is up. Joe hits a hard grounder to the infield which should have ended the game with a double play, but the runner slides hard into second base causing the throw to first to go wide.

Ted moves into the batting box – ninth inning two outs,   men on first and third, the American League still losing 5-3..

The National League pitcher works the count to 2 and 1, and then comes in with a belt-high fast ball.\

Ted remembers, " I swing – no cut down protection swing – an all-out home run swing pulling the ball to right field … it just keeps going, up, up, way up into the right field stands …Halfway down to first, seeing that the ball is going out, I stop running and start leaping and jumping and clapping my hands. I'm just so happy. I laugh out loud. I've never been so happy, and I've never seen so many happy guys. They carry me off the field, including Joe DiMaggio and Bob Feller, who had pitched early in the game and was already in his street clothes. Eddie Collins leaps out of the box seats and is there to greet me. (I've got a picture of Del Baker, the Detroit manager kissing me on the forehead. Somebody said, 'Did you kiss The Kid?' and Del Baker said, "You're damn right I did!"

Ted Williams had hit a game-winning home run in the ninth inning with two outs in an All-Star game.

On that day, July 8, 1941, at Briggs Stadium in Detroit Michigan, a legend is born.

Fast forward to the last game of the same season. against the Philadelphia Athletics Ted is hitting a rounded off .4.00, but declines his manager's offer to sit out the double-header to preserve the first .400 in eleven years.

Saturday is cold and rainy, so the game is moved to Sunday as a double0header..

. Ted singles his first time up, hits a home run, and two more singles in the first game, and breaks the loudspeaker with a double in the second game In the second game, I hit the loudspeaker horn in right field – six hits in eight times at bat raising his average to .406.

Ted doesn't remember celebrating that night, but believes he probably went out and had a chocolate milkshake.

Good times end too soon and bad times last forever. On December 7, 194, Japan bombs Pearl Harbor

Ted's mom is a volunteer for the Salvation Army, meaning she has no income. His parents are divorced. .Ted reports the money he sends to his mother as her sole support to his Draft Board, which declare Ted's mother to be a dependent and classify Ted III-A, only to change their minds a month later by reclassifying Ted I-A.

Ted goes to the Appeals Board, but they refused to change him back to III-A. (As would happen years later to Muhammad Ali and even more recently to Tom Brady, the George Goodellls of the world-- little men whose ambition far exceeds their ability, and being envious of these living legends -- masters of their trade, larger than life, singularly adored and attractive, employ bureaucratic mischief to ambush the hero they could never emulate,.

Ted, like Johnny and me – three sons with

feckless fathers,, received no guidance,, no counsel, and no support from his father. with which to do battle with his draft board, so Ted hires an attorney, who manages to get Ted a "stay of execution," – Ted was reinstated as III-A/

Ted receives his 1942 Red Sox contract, of $30,000, which he described as being, "The end of the rainbow. "

But the Goodells – Boston sportswriters – renewed their efforts to derail Ted's march toward baseball immortality by writing, "Williams ought to get in the service," instead of hiding behind his mother's apron strings.: (Joe Gordon and Joe DiMaggio of the Yankees and Stan Musial of the Cardinals get a deferral to play baseball in 1942, but Ted Williams is singled out by his draft board and the Boston press as being a reluctant patriot. (Quaker Oats cancelled their $4,000 contract with Ted,. (worth $64,000 in 2018,.)

In May, second lieutenant Ted Wi8lliams marries Doris Soule at the Navy base in Pensacola. Ted gets orders to go to Jacksonville, Florida for operational training where he sets the student gunnery record.(Is it not evidence of the genius of Ted Williams that he would be the best gunner, an expert fisherman, and the greatest hitter who ever lived?) He is waiting orders in San Francisco to be sent to fight the Japanese when the war ends,

Ted hits a 400 foot homerun the first game back in 1946, and the Red Sox are off to a fast start. (Yours truly was at the opening game at Fenway Park. Johnny Pesky hit a home run round "Pesky's Pole, " to beat the Athletics 2-1.)

The All-Star game is played in Fenway Park. Ted walks in the first inning, hits a home run, in the fourth, singles in the fifth and seventh and hits a three-run home run in the eighth

1946 is the year, the Cleveland manager installs the shift against Ted in which all the defensive players except the left fielder move to the right of second base..

Ted brought it on himself In the first game of a double-header against Cleveland that June Ted hit three home runs, the first with the bases loaded when the Sox were behind 5-0, the second with two on base to tie the game, and the third home run in the last of the ninth to win the first game 11-10."In the second game, Ted doubles to clear the bases his first time up When he comes up the second time in the second game of the double-header Lou Boudreau, the Cleveland manager, puts on his famous shift against Ted.

Other teams began to use variations of the shift Ted still won the league batting championship four times against the shift and missed the batting championship by two-tenths of a percentage point, and another time for not being up enough times officially. (With the rules now counting bases on balls as times at Ted would have won another championship.

Speaking of "what ifs," Ted lead the league in home runs in 1941 and 1942 with 37 and 36 respectively, 38 in 1946, supporting the presumption he would have averaged 37 in each of the three war years , adding 111 home runs to his 521, Considering his Korean War service at age 34 (More Goodells asserting their control over the legend), and lost games due to injuries and playing hurt the entire 1959, cost Ted another 90 home runs, for a total of 722, in 7706 at bats, Hank Aaron hit 755 home runs in 12,354 at bats and Babe Rut hit 714 in 8,399 at bats (The records of Bonds, Rodrigues, and all post- 1980 players are suspect,) Add another 10 home runs per season if Ted 's target was the short porch in right field at Yankee Stadium– 314 down the line ,and Ted could have hit over 88 more home runs.) .

The fast start in 1946, slows, then limps across the finish line in September. Meanwhile, the St. Louis Cardinals are in a playoff with the Brooklyn Dodgers. For the National League pennant, so the American League schedules a game against an American League team of all-stars in Boston, to keep the Sox fresh and ready for the World Series.

In the first inning, Ted gets hit in the elbow by a pi8tvh he was expecting to break, but didn't. The elbow swells up and turns blue, causing Ted to miss batting practice Ted never feels right during the Series, the Red Sox lose the World Series they were e expected to win, in the ninth inning of the seventh game 4-3, when the Sox relay man. held the ball a second too long before throwing home to get the Cardinal's runner..

Ted was heartbroken over the loss and his subpar performance

Ted signs his 1947 contract for $70,000, determined to "redeem" himself for the 1946 World Series, which Ted does by winning the Triple Crown – most runs scored – 123, most runs batted in –114, and highe3st batting average –343., but Joe DiMaggio wins Most Valuable Player again, this time by one point.

Joe hit .315 to Ted's .343, hit 20 home runs to Ted's 32, and drove in 107 rums to Ted's 114, but by the baseball writers' flawed logic, because the Yankees won the pennant – a measure of the team's effort, not an individual's performance, they anointed Joe MVP buy one vote.

Proving once again that the Boston baseball writers were a posse of petty, peevish, provincial, spiteful ,political, propagandists, envious of Ted like the other Goodells of the world, Boston writer Mel Webb didn't even put Ted in the top 10 on his ballot, when 10th place vote would have given Ted two points and the Most Valuable Player Award.

Looking back over his career, Ted said, "I have no excuse for the way I acted – for the things I did at certain sensational moments when I couldn't stand it anymore and just reacted -- blew up. I am sorry for them and ashamed, but would probably do them again if the conditions were the same. That's the way I am … Nothing I ever did was premeditated. Always spontaneous, boom, get it off my chest …I've always been a fierce swearer," (as was Johnny Carson and "Me.") That can be embarrassing too, but I swear to blow off steam."

Ted was fishing in the Everglades in January 1948, when his daughter Bobby-Jo was born in Boston. Ted didn't receive the news until a day later. By the time he could get a flight to Boston, Ted had been excoriated by the piranha's of the Boston press. Harold Kaese wrote, "Everybody knew where Moses was when the lights went out and everybody knows where Ted Williams was when his baby was born – he was fishing."

Kaese's mangled metaphor aside – there was fire, but no lights to go out at the time of the Exodus, no consensus when, or if, the Exodus occurred, and if the lights went out, who would have seen Moses, if there was a Moses/ Kaese's motive is clear: Character assassination of Ted, born of envy and need to sell Boston newspaper.. Another reporter called Ted a "mucker., and still another self-anointed moralist, referring to Ted's absence during the birth of Bobby Jo wrote, "You are not a nice fellow, Brother Williams. I do believe baseball and the sports pages would be better off without you. ..I wouldn't pay a dime to see you play again."

When probing Bobby Jo's mother for a story of a bitter angry mother, a reporter received the disappointing answer from her: " Bobby-Jo has Ted's eyes and my mouth."

At a different time when Ted was asked why the lure of fishing, Ted offered, " Outdoors, beautiful surroundings – trees, streams, the ocean, fresh air -- the anticipation of a strike -- the anticipation that with every cast something might happen -- the love of making a perfect cast -- the love of just being there."

The 1948 Red Sox lost a playoff game to the Cleveland Indians 8-3.

The 1949 Red Sox lost to the Yankees on the last game of the season, despite 1949 being Ted's career best - home runs – 43, runs batted in 159, but Ted missed the batting championship the last day of the season by two-tenths of a point.

While fishing down in Arkansas, Ted learns by phone that he was voted American League's Most Valuable Player. .

In 1950, Ted signs the largest contract in baseball for "$100,000.

The 1950 All-Star game is played in Comiskey Park in Chicago. Ted leads the League in home runs, already has 80 runs batted in, and with the warm months ahead, seems to be on the way to breaking his 1949 American League records, when in the first inning Pittsburg Pirates (what does land-locked Pittsburg have to do with Pirated") Ralph Kiner drives Ted against the wall to catch his long fly, shattering Ted's elbow

Ted must choose between removing the entire tip of his elbow, meaning his baseball career is kaput, or removing 13 little bone chips -- his only chance of ever playing baseball again.

Ted chooses the latter and is back in the lineup in two months. He gets four hits, one of them a home run, but the elbow isn't strong and there is still a lot of pain.

By the end of the season, the Red Sox, who had

been keeping close on the heels of the Yankees, faded into oblivion. Ted remembers, "The last two weeks of the season were miserable for me … I wasn't doing myself any good, the fans were on me, and the writers were on me …I knew that season I would never be the hitter I was before. The balls never really flew off the bat the way they had. That year there was enough weakness in it for me to know I wouldn't be hitting with authority again for a long time and with not nearly as much power. .. I struggled to hit .318 for the 1951 season. I did play 148 games which was about 60 more than I had played in 1950. I hit 30 home runs, only two more than I had hit in about half the time in 1950, (before the elbow accident in July, 1950). I drove in 126 runs, but the team was fading that year, all the way to fifth place, and in the years that followed, I would never have the opportunity to drive in so many runs again."

Despite Ted's damaged elbow, despite approaching his 34th birthday, despite his deferred status, and despite having served as a pilot 1943 -- -45, the gutless Goodells of the times on Ted's draft board called Ted into the Marines in 1952-53 for the Korean War. (Two wars took four and a half years out of his career.)"

John Kennedy, a Massachusetts Congressman, and later President, tried to help, Ted but said he couldn't.

Ted will never realize – nor would Mohammad Ali – that by making examples of Ted and Ali, the old money class demonstrates for all to see, that no matter how much money Ted and Ali would accrue, and/or how famous and popular they become, they are forever precluded from sitting at the table of the privileged and powerful who control them. So, for example when Bush II was faced with fighting in Vietnam, Bush I, managed to get Junior sent to the Texas Air National Guard, where the sons of the rich Texans, played airplanes. Junior even deserted his unit during wartime. Had he been from Ted's or Ali's class, he would have been shot, but Bush II is honorably discharged, never having spent a day in combat.)

The doctor who administers Ted's physical says, "The arms' all right," (Years later another army doctor announces son of millionaire Trump Senior, one Donald Trump has a medical deferment -- bone spurs, which surprises college athlete Donald, who later couldn't remember which foot it had been.

Six games after the season started, Ted becomes a captain in the Marines as a fighter pilot.

That last game in Boston, they declare "Ted Williams Day". Boston baseball writer Dave Egan, willing to write anything to sell a newspaper, asks in his cancerous column. "Why are we having a day for this guy?'"

Ted, distrustful of the sincerity of the fickle public's emotional displays, is a reluctant folk hero, declaring, "I don't want them to have any days for me either. I don't want to be obliged."

The Boston Mayor proclaims "Ted Williams Day" They give Ted a Cadillac, and a memory book signed by 400.000 fans. All the fans hold hands and sing "Auld Lang Syne."

It had to touch Ted, because he admits afterward that he took his baseball cap out of his back pocket and held it up – he insists he did NOT tip it – but pointing to the left-field stands, proclaims, "This is the greatest day of my life. I'll always remember it. It's a day every ballplayer looks for, and one I thought I'd never have. I never thought when I came to the Red Sox 14 years ago that they were such a wonderful organization. They've been wonderful to me."

The opposing team that night is the Detroit

Tigers. In the seventh inning, the score is tied 3-3. With two men out, and Red Sox center fielder Dom DiMaggio on base. It will be Ted's last time up – maybe his last time ever – the end of his legendary career.

As testimony to his genius for concentration, fifteen years later, Ted recalls the pitcher's name - Dizzy Dean and the pitch   he threw -- a low inside curve – "a pretty good pitch and I hit it into the right-field bullpen winning the game 5-3.".

Of such feats legends are consummated.

Ted invites his people to the party he throws at the Hotel Kenmore.-- cab drivers, bartenders, bat boys, cops – bellhops.

"I had to think at the time that it was my last home run in the big league baseball. I'm 33 years old. I would be 35 when I got back. Chances are I wouldn't ever play again.'

As events would have it, not only was it likely to have been Ted's last day as a baseball player, but his last day alive.

As he recounts in *My Turn at Bat*, Ted's is flying a combat mission over North Korea attacking a large troop encampment. Ted loses track of the plane in front of him and by swinging out to relocate him, Ted is now flying too low over the target.

"Sure as hell I get hit with small arms fire. When I pull up out of my run, all the red lights are on and the damn plane begins to shake … The fuel warning and fire warning lights are on…I'm in serious trouble. Suddenly there's a plane behind me … He comes up close. I see he's pointing like mad trying to show me I'm leaking fuel. He signals with his thumb, 'Let's get up …Altitude is a safety factor. The thinner air helps in case of fire and another 10,000 feet lets you glide 35-40 miles if the engine fails … I've taken off my leg strap … I'm going

to have to bail out … I get up to 18,000 feet … From the target to the base is about 15 minutes. Suddenly, we are over the field nearer the target. It's a madhouse -- 60 planes in from the mission, all low on fuel.. But all I had eyes for was that little field. I start to make my break on a fairly tight turn, when *fffuumum!* – a big explosion. One of the wheel doors has blown off. Now there's fire and smoke under the plane … I come in
about 223 miles per hour, twice as fast as ordinary. … With 30 feet of fire streaming from the plane, the villagers living next to the field are running to beat hell. I pull the emergency wheel latch, but only one wheel drops down. I hit flush and skid up the runway -- No dive brakes and no flaps to slow the plane. For more than a mile I skid ripping, and tearing up the runway -- sparks flying."

" I see the fire truck. I press the brakes so hard I almost break my ankle -- all the time screaming, "When is this dirty S.O.B. going to stop? … Further up the runway the plane starts sliding toward a second fire truck which takes off to get out of the way, dust flying behind it. I stop right at the end of the runway. The canopy won't open. I hit the emergency ejector. Everything is on fire except the cockpit. Boy I just dive out and kind of somersault. Two Marines are there to grab me. I take my helmet and slam it on the ground. I'm so mad.

Generally after a close call like that they ground you, but we are hurting for pilots, so I'm back flying missions the next day.

After 39 missions and being hospitalized for pneumonia, Ted is "mustered out" because of a ear problem, for which Ted has to sign a medical waiver.

When Ted gets to San Francisco, Ford Frick, Baseball Commissioner calls Ted to throw out the first ball at the All-Star came in Cincinnati. Then, Fred

Corcoran, Ted's business manager calls; to urge Ted to get back to playing baseball, arguing, There's still two months left in the season. Everybody wants you back.. I think you ought to try to play this year."

Ted answers, "Hell, Fred. It's the middle of July. The Red Sox aren't going anywhere. I'm not ready to play baseball. Mr. Yawkey says I can do what I feel like doing. I feel like fishing. I'm going fishing."

Corcoran counters, "You're not a fisherman. You're a ballplayer. Baseball is your business."

On about the eighth or ninth pitch during Ted's first day of batting practice, Ted hits one into the center field bleachers.

Joe Cronin, the Red Sox's general manager is reported to have said, "Ted, nobody's hit one out there all year." (Of such feats, legends ripen.

Ted's first day back at Fenway Park, in the eighth inning Ted pinch hits a home run over the right center-field fence. Ted had hit a home run to win the game he last played in Fenway Park before going off to fight in the Korean War, and now hits a home run on his first day back at Fenway Park. (Of such extraordinary performances, Ted's legend accrues disciples.)

For the next 37 games, Ted hit .407, 13 home runs, -- a home run every seven times at bat, and had a slugging percentage of .901. (Babe Ruth's career slugging percentage tops the list at .690. Ted finishes second at .634, Lou Gehrig third at 632 -- Joe DiMaggio, .579, Willie Mays, .557, and Mickey Mantlr .557.)

On the first day of spring training the next year, Ted falls coming in for a line drive and breaks his collar bone – the Second World War, the elbow, the Korean War, and now a broken collarbone! (Any connection between Ted's broken bones and his brother Danny breaking his arm by throwing an orange due to his leukemia of his bone marrow?) Ted misses36 game

In April, Ted states in an article for the *Saturday Evening Post* that he is retiring at the end of the season.

"I'm hurt. I'm tired. I'm disgusted -- mad at the writers – mad at everybody. I have every intention of packing it in … "My marriage break-up is part of it. …

Back in the lineup on May 7, in Detroit, Ted goes eight for nine in a double-header, and plays every game -- 117 – for the rest of the season, hits .345, but because Ted didn't have the required 400 at bats – he had only 386, he wasn't eligible to win the batting title.

"The pitchers were walking me so damn much." (Back then, walks didn't count as times at bat.)

In September, Ted retired,.

That July, Ted is sitting on a bench in Baltimore waiting for his train to Boston. This stranger comes up and says, "You're not really going to quit, are you?"

Without even looking up, Ted Answers. "Yeah, I think I am."

The stranger's name is Ed Mifflin, a "two-legged baseball encyclopedia," telling Ted facts and statistics Ted had not considered. For example, if Ted retires in September, he would not even be in the top ten in all-time home runs. On the other hand, if he continues to play, he could reach 500 home runs -- fourth place behind Ruth, Foxx, and Ott, be in the top five all-time in RBI's (runs batted in) and get 4,000 total bases – the accumulation of all the hits he has gotten – a home run counts four and a single counts one.)

So while weighing whether to retire or play, instead of going to Spring training that February, Ted stayed down on the Keys fishing.

The year before Ted signed a $100,000 contract – the biggest in baseball,

On May 9, 1955, Doris won her divorce -- $50,000, alimony, $125 a week, a $50,000 house, thereby convincing Ted he couldn't afford not to go back to work for the Boston Red Sox.

On May 13, Ted signs a contract for $98,000 with the Red Sox. hurry and can't afford to wait for the calluses.

He hits a home run his first day back,, .356 for the season, but not the batting title because he was credited with only 320 times at bat. (Ted was walked 110 times) The rules committee changed the rule, but not until AFTER Ted lost the batting title due to a technicality. .

The closest the Red Sox came in the next five years to win the American League pennant is third place. With the exception of 1948 and 1954, when the Cleveland Indians won the AL, (The Red Sox lost a one-game playoff in 1948, and on the last game of season to the Yankees in 1949,) and 1959 , when the Chicago White Sox won, From 1947 to 1960, when Ted retired, the New York Yankees won the American League Championship –seven out of ten years.

Ted went to spring training in 1957 thinking it would be his last year.

" I started the season mad, and I finished mad. I didn't say two words to the Boston writers all year and in between had the most amazing season any near-forty year-old ever had … We went to Cleveland. It's one of those cold, rotten nights. I hit a home run the first time up, and a home run the second time up. I ask manager Higgins to take me out -- the weather was so bad He said, "What for? You might hit another." Sure enough I hit another home run setting a major league record – it was the second time that year I'd hit three home runs in one game. "

In September, Ted hit four home runs in four consecutive times at bat to tie another record.

After being "holed up" for 17 days that

September with another chest infection, Ted pinch-hits for a homer, then walks, hits a second home run –the next day hits a grand-slam, after which the Yankee pitchers walk Ted three straight times. The next day Ted walks before hitting his fourth home run of the series -- reaching base sixteen straight times – all against the New York Yankees. (Of such feats diehard baseball fans trip over themselves to bear witness to the living legend aka, Ted Williams'

"It's that kind of year where every move I make is a headline,"   I "

In the spring of 1959, Ted is swinging a bat in his back yard in Islamorada on the Florida Keys, The next day, he feels pain in his neck He's take in traction for three weeks.

In *My Turn at Bat*, Ted describes the 1959 season: "When I finally get out of the hospital and back with the team, I'm no good to anybody. I have a miserable year – the worst of my career I can barely turn my neck to look at the pitcher, thrashing around all year near .250."

After the "59" season ends, Red Sox owner, Tom Yawkey calls Ted to his office, hinting Ted should retire, but there is no way, Ted Williams is going to retire after the worst year of his career. Ted volunteers to a pay cut of "$35,000 signing to play the 1960 season for :$90,000.

In the first game of the season, Ted hits t a 500-foot home run, Ted's 493th home run tying him with Gehrig, behind Ruth, Foxx and Ott. The next day he hits another home run. During one stretch, he's hitting a home run every seven times at bat.   The Sporting News votes Ted *The Player of the Decade.*

The Red Sox are in Fenway for the last series of the season, and Ted's last game.

The headline in that morning's reads, "What Will We Do Without Ted?"

Ted doesn't take batting practice. The wind is blowing in -- a dark, dreary, cold, threatening day by game time.

The first time Ted come up, the Baltimore pitcher walks Ted on four straight pitches. The second time up, Ted hits a fly to right center, which on another day, would have been a home run, but not today. The air is just too heavy; the same fate greets a fifth inning drive, which instead of being a home run. ends in the Baltimore centerfielder's glove at the 380 sign, (The day by now is so dark, oppressive, and gloomy, they had to turn the lights on.)

When the first Red Sox hitter gets on base, Ted comes to bat, "Feeling the chills up and down my spine, thinking how much I want to put one out of the park on my last game and my last time at bat. but I know the odds are stacked against me."

First pitch: Ball one. Ted notices that the Baltimore pitcher "humps up as if he were going to try to fire the ball by me. And gee, here comes a ball I should hit a mile, but I miss the son of a gun. I don't completely miss very often and I don't know yet how I missed that pitch …This time I try to be a little quicker – hit it a little better -- put a little extra on it…"

The ball's flight fights the wind – two physical forces in a battle fit for Greek gods…the outcome settled only when the sphere propelled by a god of humankind reaches its destination, to wit, the Red Sox bull pen."

The 10,454 people in Fenway Park who braved the weather that day, rise as one in chorus of jubilation celebrating the victory of their humanity's god over a god of the Universe's forces.

The Effect of Ted's Mother's Toxic Breast Milk on Ted

Ted's mother -- mother *in absentia*, volunteered 24/7 as a Salvation Army worker saving the souls of the "street people" – denizens of the downtrodden slums of San Diego, but couldn't find time to feed and care for Ted and his younger brother Danny.

Ted recalls, "My mother was gone all day and half the night working the streets for the Salvation Army. I also didn't see much of my dad. He had a little photographic shop taking passport pictures and photos of sailors with their girls. He wouldn't get home until nine, or ten o'clock. …Danny and I fed ourselves.

Ted's mother insisted that Ted march with the Salvation Army band.

"Oh how I hated that! I never wore a uniform, but I was right at the age when kids start worrying about what other kids think, especially a gawky introverted kid like me. I was just so ashamed … "

Ted remembers that people called his mother "the "Angel of Tijuana'" and "Salvation May …"Many nights my brother Danny and I would be out on our porch past ten o'clock waiting for one of our parents to come home …I was maybe eight at the time and Danny was six. I know the neighbors must have thought it was terrible for us, but kids don't think in those terms. They think about getting inside and getting something to eat"

Ted grew to realize that his mother had a lot of traits that made Ted "cringe"…. "She was religious to the point of being domineering, and so narrow-minded!"

Without a father with whom to relate, by default, Ted always felt closer to his mother. "I had to do right by her, always feeling she was alone, and knowing for years afterward how hard she had worked with nothing to show for it. Until the day she died, it always embarrassed me. God knows I respected her and loved her ."

Ted went to spring training in 1957 thinking it would be his last year. He played an exhibition game that spring in San Diego – the first time he'd been home in five years. **My mother was going to be at the game, but she got sick and couldn't make it. In all my career she probably saw me play only five or six times, but never as a big leaguer. She was always so wrapped up in the Salvation Army.**

Ted , Johnny, and I each had toxic relationships with our mothers. Ted recalls, "My mother was gone all day and half the night working the streets for the Salvation Army…. They called her the "Angel of Tijuana" and "Salvation May," but the thing a kid remembers is that he never saw his mother very much"

" I was always closer to my mother … always feeling I had to do right by her…" (Was there a connection between his mother being "Salvation May," and Ted's dedication to the Jimmy Fund, his love of children, (other than his own), and his "adoption" of some of the children hospitalized with terminal illnesses?)

Ted is torn between his love for his mother and the pain her negligence causes him

"I want people to say, "There goes Ted Williams, the greatest hitter who ever lived." (Ted hoping that by winning the love of the fans he would feel the love which had proven unwinnable from his mother.)

But Ted's -- the "Kid's"-- goal of being the "greatest hitter who ever lived,'" – naïve, vulnerable, raised without grooming and social skills, absent parental tutoring as to the ways of the world, honest to a fault – is on a collision course with war-tested word warriors of the Boston sport's press, whose mortgage payments depend on using Ted to sell newspapers.

The Boston press's daily reports of Ted's encounters with a ball thrown toward him at 90+ mph, from only 60 feet six inches away, changing direction, with .45 seconds to react, paid for their Mercedes, their beer, and their mistresses.

The best hitters fail 66.7% of the time. Ted was the best of the best.

Wars, murders, bank robberies, fires, and rape sell newspapers.. So does hammering hero Ted for his 66.7% failures at bat, and the personality flaws in a kid who was raised by neighbors, a playground director, and his high school baseball coach.

Ted's hurt goes much deeper. The Boston press's attacks on Ted's hitting skills is an assault on Ted's ability to win his mother's love the only way he knew how -- becoming the greatest hitter ever. His temper-tantrum counter-attacks told us so.

As a little boy, Ted excused his mother's dereliction of duty. As a man-child he could not forgive the predatory Boston press and the fair-weather Boston fans for their hurtful insults, taunts, and boos. He would not reward their duplicity by tipping his cap to their applause following his homeruns. It was a matter of principle, and Ted Williams was a person of inexorable principle.

Ted, Johnny and I had weak, feckless fathers, making our relationships with our mothers – sink or swim -- We three sank.

Ted acknowledged, "My dad and I were never close." When having problems with the press, the draft board, his wives and children, Ted wished he had a dad like his teammate Bobby Doerr's dad – a dad who Ted could trust and advise him – be in Ted's corner.

Ted, without his mother' love, was insecure, shy, seeking the safety of solitude – going fishing -- avoiding social events and parties whenever possible, once even when he was the guest to be honored.

Ted's first friends were the man across the street in San Diego, the Playground Director around the corner, later, the Red Sox club house boy, and a state trooper.

Ted confided, "A girl looked at me twice, and I'd run the other way." Johnny, Carson, the consummate jokester and court jester, described his participation at parties as "grin and bear it." As a teen, I too crossed the street to avoid girls.

Without the unconditional love and trust of our mothers, how would we ever love and trust another woman. We didn't. EVER!

Yet, we three, absent the experience of having bonded with our mothers, were nevertheless, compelled – propelled – to try to bond with a woman, unaware that that our very inexperience precluded us from obtaining a working knowledge of the needs and wants of women, in turn rendering us "impossible to live with," as each of our four wives would independently attest – describe us as "irascible explosive, short-fused, verbally abusive, foul-mouthed scape-goating, sometimes cruel, and habitually making the present wife pay for past sins of our mothers," with interest compounded daily..

Ted, Johnny, and I, without the unconditional love of a mother developed dysfunctional self-destructive personalities, which repulsed the very social belonging we coveted, in turn, guaranteeing us the loneliness and sense of abandonment we so feared.

.We three each had four wives. (Louise was Ted's fourth in every way except the piece of paper).

With no mother as a model, Ted's wives were trophies, as Ted may have been to them – beauty and sex to satisfy the beast's longing for a mother's love.

With no model of how a husband treats his wife, Ted expected his wives to adjust to him. Three wives declined. Only Louise consented, but then she died.

Ted. Johnny, and I, each a victim of bad parenting, became bad dads. In Ted's case, Bobby Jo , was likely a Borderline Personality, Claudia, a success for having "divorced " Ted, and John Henry, a Psychopathic Personality, cheated his way through college, exploited Ted for profit , became involved in a series of "shady business deals," and in a sick perversion of the Oedipus Complex, had dead Ted's head .

Louise's unconditional love won where beauty and conditional love failed." Had Ted at last found the true love denied him, first by his mother, then by three wives, too many fucking flings (literally) , and millions of baseball fans?

The answer went to the grave -- Louise died on August 10, 1993, following surgery.

How Ted's Three Wives (Plus One) Each Failed The "Mom Test"

In May, 1944, second lieutenant Ted Wi8lliams marries Doris Soule, daughter of a fishing guide in Minnesota, who Ted met while on a fishing trip.

They divorce e in 1954, "Doris and I had gotten on different paths, that's all. I hadn't lived in the house in Miami very long before I went to Korea. I wasn't back three months before I moved out for good. I guess you would have to say that as my life away from home – my baseball—got bigger, my life at home got smaller. It happens.

On May 9, 1955, Doris won her divorce. She got $50,000, $125 a week, and a $50,000 house"

Ted tries marriage again in 1961, to an attractive blond named Lee Howard from Chicago. She too was divorced.

Ted's mother dies a month before Ted's marriage. (His brother Danny, died a year earlier of leukemia. John Henry, Ted's son, also died of leukemia.

(Ted had a history of broken bones – elbow, collar bones, ankle related to common pool of DNA?)

Ted attended both funerals alone, without Lee.. (Had Lee known of Ted's shame of his family, his heritage, especially of his mother, Lee might have understood why Ted went alone. Lee might also have remembered Ted seldom talked about his life in San Diego, nothing about his father, and brother and about his mother only in the context of how much he hated having to march in Salvation Army parades with her.

Lee might have connected the dots, but didn't, bemoaning, "You'd have thought when she died it would have a natural time to talk about her. It just didn't happen."

We weren't suited. We couldn't get along. Ted had trouble understanding women …" (Yes indeed, he did. So did Johnny Carson. So did I and for the same reasons. It's inevitable of sons who never understood their mothers. Johnny Carson never understood his mother's cruelty – why, no matter how much he tried to please her, he received not so much as a "thank you." Ted never understood why his mother mothered the "street people" of San Diego, but not him/

Meanwhile,, Ted's marriage to Delores is also kaput. The reason is the same. Too many personal profane tirades without probable cause and with no apologies.

As author Montville noted, "He (Ted) had married his first love, Doris," who gave birth to Bobby Jo."That didn't work." (for Doris, Bobby Jo, or Ted). He next marries Lee Howard the actress and model, for love. That didn't work. He marries Delores out of necessity – she was pregnant with John Henry. That marriage ends. Same reason: Too many personal profane tirades without probable cause and with no apologies.

Enter Louise, the antithesis of Ted's previous wives – no beauty queen here. Louise had taken up occupancy in the past. Visitors thought she was Ted's housekeeper. She was older than Ted, but looked much older. Having been a long-time Florida Keys neighbor of Ted's and widow for many of those years, Louise had lost out to Lee and Delores, to Ted's many encounters of a sexual kind, and one-night stands, but through all of those episodes of heartbreak, Louise's love and loyalty never wavered

Plain "Jane" Louise persists when the *Vogue* model, Hollywood actress, and Miss Vermont had jumped ship. (In his book, Montville makes the convincing argument that Louise's unconditional love" won where beauty and conditional love failed.)"She gave Ted's life order. She cleaned his clothes, cooked his meals, and poured his cocktails."

In 1993, Louise is a reluctant companion on their annual summer fishing trip to Canada. (She's been suffering with a painful bowel obstruction.)

On August 10, 1993, the hospital calls.. Ted is out in the middle of the river fishing. The message: Ted must come to the hospital; ASAP.

After Louise's death in 1993, Ted never visits the river again.

Louise's daughter describes her mother's relationship with Ted as being like Katharine Hepburn's 50 - year love affair with Spencer Tracy. Ted and Louise live together, bonded by mutual love, but never married. Louise was the one and only "woman who could take his shit," put up with his infidelities, and his disappearances, to wit the only woman who loved Ted unconditionally.

Ted's Children Sacrificed on the Altar of Their Famous Father's Fame

The wife of one of Ted's Korean War buddies noted during visits that Ted was constantly telling Bobby Jo what to do and how to do it -- "Sit up straight"…"Put your hands in your lap at the dinner table," begging the question how did Ted become "Mr. Manners" when there is no evidence the Williams family ever sat down to a meal together, no evidence either that Ted's parents cared enough for Ted and Danny to teach them to "sit up straight" or "put your hands in your lap at the dinner table.

Bobby Jo was caught between "a rock" (her Draconian father) and a "hard place" (her mother who was too drunk to care,)

Lee remembers, that when Bobby Jo came to visit – she was 12 and 13 at that time, Ted "would get mad at her for the smallest thing -- things that kids do …Lee would take her shopping to get her out of the house … wondering if it would have been better if she had been a boy…

Ted's dream was that Bobby Jo would get the college education Ted had wished for himself. Instead, Bobby Jo gets pregnant at age 16 or 17, a patient at the University of Pennsylvania psychiatric treatment center, (As did Johnny's son Rick become a patient at The Bellevue Psychiatric Hospital in New York), got an abortion, had a history of promiscuity, and suicide attempts, and elopes at age 18 with the son of a racing form distributor, thereby earning her father's same shame and disappointment he felt toward his own mother and father.

In public, Ted sadly concluded, "Kids, break your heart." (Yes, Ted, but so did your mother and father break yours.)

Ted's other daughter, Claudia, 25 years younger than Bobby Jo, and even younger than Bobby Jo's children, hearing the stories about her half-sister's self-destructive life – Bobby Jo's teen-age marriage and divorce, her perpetual promiscuities, drug abuse, mental institutionalization, applies to the prestigious/elitist Middlebury College, (famous for its foreign language department). Claudia is reportedly rejected three times.

Ted calls Middlebury College. Now, it is Claudia, who turns down Middlebury, arguing," If all it took to be accepted is a call from my famous father, I don't want to go to that kind of college." (She graduates from Springfield College in Springfield, Massachusetts, known for its PE department, teaches English in Germany, and becomes a tri-athlete.)

Ted's third child and only son, John Henry is to Ted what Johnny's son "Rick" was to Johnny. Let us count the ways.

In Ted's purported Old World sensibilities, sons are valued and daughters are de-valued, or is John Henry's most favored family status gratuitously given by his misogynist father? In either case, certainly Claudia is all too aware of her second-class status as daughter of Ted Williams and sister to John Henry.

John Henry made his uneventful debut at age one, hanging around the dugout when his father was managing the Washington Senators – "uneventful" as few of the players associated a one year old with their 50-ish manager. ("Me" again. Sorry for the interruption, I also had four wives, poor relationships with my children – four from three wives. and fathered a son in my 50's. Totally scary).

John Henry, now 13, is a batboy at the Old Timer's game in 1982, in Fenway Park.

After the divorce, Delores moves back to the family farm in Vermont, giving John Henry and Claudia a taste of the good life in rural Vermont and the constancy of grandparents. John Henry attends high school at Vermont Academy, a private school for kids of wealth and privilege.

One day, a video game money box is missing and an estimated $150 – well not so much missing, but in the possession of John Henry, who, in turn, is in the custody of his mother on the way to the principal's office, facing automatic expulsion for the theft.

Although caught with the loot, and unwillingly turned in by his mother, John Henry's apology to the principal and the return of his heist, suffice to stay his expulsion.

His senior year of high school, while attempting to cremate a dead farm cat as he had seen his grandfather do, John Henry nearly cremates himself, sustaining severe burns to his arms and chest, requiring hospitalization at the Boston Shriner's Burns Institute. John Henry eventually recovers, returns to Vermont Academy, makes up the work, and graduates with Ted and Louise in attendance.

Ted and John Henry pick Bates College, a Division III school in Maine from the short list including Babson and Bowdoin. The Bates baseball coach tells father and son about the two week tryouts in the spring and that there would be cuts. When Ted arrives to pick up John Henry for spring break, John Henry asks the coach if he and Ted could use the field house for batting practice.

The observing coach is not impressed. He cuts

John Henry, tells him to play more baseball, and try again next year.

There wouldn't be a next year. John Henry flunks out. The next stop is the University of Maine, a Division I school with the reputation of being a New England college baseball powerhouse, coached by Ted's long-time friend and coach at Ted's baseball camp, for 15 years, John Winkin.

John Henry shows up for the tryouts with his own bats and bag of balls, heads for the varsity practice field, and is told to go to the JV field by the coach, John Henry does exactly the same the next day, but this time he leaves and never comes back.

Winkin notes, "You had to watch him like a hawk….I thought he was a sneaky guy."

John Henry drops out, claims he played semi-pro ball in California, tries acting, playing for the Toronto Blue Jays, and then returns to the University of Maine, where he makes no friends and influences few people -- the consensus being John Henry is "stuck up and a prima donna." (Or, a Psychopathic Personality?)

The exception is Maine State trooper Rodney Nichols, who John Henry meets while waiting for President George Bush I to arrive on Air Force One for a vacation in Maine.

Nichols is soon accompanying John Henry on his weekend trips to Citrus Hills, Florida, where John Henry is now selling home sites. Of course, they stay in the big house with Ted and play golf with Ted, who Nichols claims gets along better with him than Ted does with John Henry. "If the two of them didn't holler at each other once during a day it was a rare day." (Recall Johnny Carson's rocky relationship with his son, Rick, and their near fistacuffs at the *The Tonight Show's* anniversary party on the *Queen Mary* in 1987.)

Nichols attends John Henry's graduation from

Maine with Ted, Claudia, and other friends. John Henry fulfills Ted's dream by becoming the first of his family to graduate from college. (Not exactly, for when John Henry opens the folder presented him, he discovers there is no diploma). The College had let him go through the ceremony, but he is one class short of the required number of courses, a fact John Henry, knew, or should have known, but deceived Ted that there must have been a "mix-up."

Later, Nichols tells Montville that John Henry, signed up for a summer course, but never went to class. Instead he bought "a miniature walkie-talkie" system in a New York spy store. "A kid I know sat out in the car and read the answers on the final exam to John Henry sitting in class taking the exam. That's how he got his diploma. (More evidence John Henry is without a conscience – A Psychopathic Personality?)

John Henry didn't just show the diploma to Ted, but made a production of it by placing it in a large box with pictures, and all 'kinds of stuff." (Ted never knew the truth.)

His senior year, John Henry made his first foray into the sports memorabilia business, soon forming Grand Slam Marketing, Major League Memorabilia and the Ted Williams Card Company, before opening. The Ted Williams Store, in January, 1994, begging the question, was John Henry helping or exploiting his father?

Ted is recovering from his third stroke (the big one) in February 1994, when, in July, John Henry promotes the Ted Williams Store with a sale of a lithograph signed by Ted, Dominic DiMaggio, Johnny Pesky, Bobby Doerr, and Eddie Pellagrini.

Ted, his vision severely impaired from the strokes, looking "fatigued," and walking with a cane, had come up from Florida for the event. All the signers were present along with 600 ticket holders. A short time later the store closes as abruptly as it had opened.

That summer Ted interviews and hires George Carter, a former marine and cop, as his live-in 24/7 male nurse.

December, 1994, absent from said residence -- the "love of his life" Louise Kaufman, her replacement Lynette Simon, and Ted's long-time secretary Stacia Gerow, are all fired, or driven away by John Henry who arrives, and   appoints himself *de facto* guardian of the person and estate of his faltering father.

"John Henry rules with the air of privilege that his famous dad never had -- workers thought John Henry arrogant, greedy, and worst of all, incompetent."

For his part, John Henry is convinced they are all thieves.

George Carter regrets he never told Ted how "bad" John Henry was. "We all knew how much Ted loved his son no matter how many times John Henry disappointed his father."

John Henry's business plan is simple: Sell Ted's signature on as many bats, balls, shirts and whatevers as possible – Ted autographs. John Henry sells.

Delores, wife number three and John Henry's and Claudia's mother , emboldened by the death of Louise and Ted's stroke, and with her son in charge, invites herself down from Vermont much to Ted's dismay -- sunbathes nude, wears scandalous dresses, makes lewd remarks to other visitors and staff, and once arriving with a wedding dress announcing she and Ted are getting married again. (Ted might well have had another stroke, but didn't.)

That Thanksgiving, returning from an "exercise walk," Ted falls in his driveway, breaking the same shoulder he broke in the All-Star game. He falls again in 1997, this time his dog "Slugger" knocks him over. Ted had to have his hip replaced.   .

     The autograph/memorabilia business begins to profit. John Henry is selling Ted's autograph as fast as he can get his dad to affix his signature, never mind how challenging and exhausting the task is to Ted.

     Meanwhile, John Henry gets involved in a number of shady deals, lawsuits, and scandals.

     The 1999 All-Star game is moved to Fenway Park because the new ballpark in Milwaukee would not be completed in time. Thirty-three nominees for the All-Century Team are flown in for the ceremony and announced to the crowd one by one -- Cobb, Ruth, Gehrig, DiMaggio, and Mantle had all died, leaving Ted Williams, the oldest of the living All-Century Team

     In Ted's former *Field of Dreams* , he throws out the first pitch.

     Montville writes of that magical moment: "He could be caught one last time in this late curtain call for a generation …but there was still time for one more wave, a goodbye, a wet-eyed standing ovation. He is wrapped in the flag, wrapped in all the sweet, childhood memories of baseball, in the promise of youth, the sadness of old age, wrapped in noise and emotion. He is elevated to some level of secular American sainthood …With the Citgo sign pulsating behind the center field stand, a giant No.9 stenciled into the outfield grass, and the ancient theatre shaking on its landfill foundation, Williams stands in front of the mound …the players around him would be only so many supporting actors from the drama of Ted Williams Day". And he would remove his cap – yes he did – and wave it at everyone in triumph – his Hitternet cap." (Ah, and there's the rub, for in appearing to have convinced Ted to wear the Hitternet cap, instead of a Red Sox cap, John Henry once again incurred the public's wrath for using his famous father to promote John Henry's business interests -- more evidence of John Henry's psychopathology.)

In the end, the consensus of millions of Ted's fans, the national and international baseball public, and other players, is that Ted Williams had fulfilled his boyhood goal of becoming "the 'greatest hitter who ever lived" -- a legend in his own time – a hero's hero, who defied the gods by being a motherless son, heir of a feckless father, a victim of poverty, and racial discrimination, and who defied the etched- in-stone odds that a baseball pitcher wins 72.5% of the time.

Death being the final arbiter, ordered that at 8:49 AM, July 5. 2002, Ted Williams beloved by millions, worshipped by many, whose genius with a baseball bat did that which Michelangelo had done with a paint brush, Mozart with piano keys, and Shakespeare with a quill, died alone, without family, friends, or fans in the Emergency Room at Citrus Memorial Hospital in Inverness, Florida at age 83, never having felt the one thing he wanted over all else – his mother's love.

…Ten thousand eyes were on him as he wiped his hands with dirt, five thousand tongues applauded as he wiped them on his shirt. Then when the writhing pitcher ground the ball into his hip, defiance gleamed in Teddy's eyes, a sneer curled Teddy's lip. And now the leather-covered sphere came hurling through the air, and Teddy stood a-watching it in haughty grandeur there. Close by the sturdy batsman the ball unheeded sped, "That aint my style," said Teddy -- "Strike one," the umpire said. From the benches black with people went up a muffled roar, like the beating of the storm waves on the stern and distant shore. "Kill him! Kill the

umpire" someone shouted in the stand -- And it's likely they'd have killed him had not Teddy raised his hand. With the smile of Christian charity, Teddy's visage shone. He stilled the rising tumult and bade the game go on. He signaled the pitcher, and once more the spheroid flew. But Teddy still ignored it, and the umpire said, "Strike two." "Fraud" cried the maddened thousands and the echo answered, "Fraud" But one scornful look from Teddy and the audience was awed. They saw his face grow stern and cold, they saw his muscles strain. And they knew that Teddy wouldn't let that ball go by again. The sneer is gone from Teddy's lip, his teeth are clenched in hate. He pounds with cruel vengeance his bat upon the plate. And now the pitcher holds the ball, and now he lets it go. And now the air is shattered by the force of Teddy's blow. Oh, somewhere in this land of ours, the sun is shining bright, The band is playing somewhere, and somewhere hearts are light, And somewhere men are laughing, and somewhere children shout, And they're going wild in Fenway Park, 'cause Teddy hit one out. "—Dick Flavin

Me -- Last & Least Being the Most Wounded of We Three Sparrows

The first time my mother visits me at the foster home in the Brookline section of Boston, is the last time I ever saw her. She just left me at the front door -- no hug – no kiss – no good-by – no telling me when she'd be back – I guess because she knew she never was coming back.

I wanted to ask her, "Why are you making me live with a man, I've never seen before, who doesn't like me and I don't like him? What did I do to make you hate me so much?

No birthday card, no Christmas card. No phone call… I'm only four.

Ten years later, I'm standing in my grandmother's living room..(She wasn't my real grandmother because she had adopted my father.)

The phone rings."Hello,"

My grandmother listens, says nothing, then hangs up, turns to me and says, "Your mother's dead," and leaves the room. (It would be years later, that on each occasion love was lost, stolen, or forsaken, that grief's abundance would conjoin with the progeny of grief's maternal ancestor)

-- No hug, no kiss. No chance to cry. Just, "Your mother's dead." (Come to think of it, I never remember my ersatz grandmother hugging or kissing me. I do remember her hovering over me while I recited that terrifying, child-abusing, Marquis de Sade, prayer, "…if I should die before. I wake, I pray the Lord my soul to take," my grandmother making sure I listed her first on the list of "God blesses," or be sent back to the foster home from which she rescued me.

Ah and there's the rub, for my father's seemingly benign adoption, when compounded with my mother's unseemly family history, gave heir to a lineage of troubled offspring and dysfunctional families -- for six generations and counting.

My mother's Birth Certificate, first seen by me sometime after my father died in 1987, reads: "<u>Child's Mother's Maiden Name:</u> Pauline Carver. <u>Child's Father:</u> Edward A. Smythe. <u>Child's name:</u> Janet Smythe – born November 15, 1918, in Framingham, Massachusetts."

Three problems: First, my mother's mother and father were not married until 1921, when my mother was three. Second, my mother made her debut (No debutante here) with the sobering sobriquet of "Sister," meaning, to cover up my mother's *de facto* illegitimacy, her parents convince her she's her mother's baby sister!

Her subsequent five brothers would call her "Aunt Janet," and everyone else, including my father, at least at first, called her "Sister." (Women in Massachusetts in 1918, would probably still toss and turn in their sleep haunted by Hawthorne's 1850's warning that Hester Pyrnne's scarlet letter "A" is their fate, if but an intrusive sperm away.)

Problem Three. Mr. Smythe is really Edwin A. Teschner, first generation German, Phillips Academy graduate -- "Dutch" -- for "Deutsch" -- Harvard graduate. and captain of the Harvard track team in 1916-7 (?) when track was a major college sport. (He may even have been a world record holder -- 9.5 in 100 yard dash before world records were kept.)

On the Birth Certificate, Edward A. Smythe's occupation is listed as, "Soldier U.S.A.," his birthplace Wilkeyville, NY, and the current residence of Mr. & Mrs. Edward Smythe is listed as Marlboro, Massachusetts.,

Putting the pieces of the puzzle together, I infer that my maternal grandmother Pauline Carver, twin sister to Paul Carver, from a long line of New England Baptist ministers, perhaps going back to a John Carver, passenger on the *Mayflower,* kin to the New Hampshire Brewsters and, reportedly John Philip Sousa, is a student at Framingham Normal School -- a teachers' training college in Framingham, Massachusetts, now called Framingham State University.

Woops! Pauline Carver, unmarried heiress to centuries of New England Baptist Preachers, is impregnated by Ed Smythe, Harvard graduate, track star, and US soldier.

Not wanting their education to be irrelevant to such pedestrian problems as panic, the Smythes (really Teschners) entangle the illegitimate birth of my mother in a web of intrigue in which my mother becomes "Sister" – baby sister of her mother and her father's sister-in-law. (Oh what a tangled web we weave when we but practice to conceal what we conceive.)

Just when you thought the apples from my family tree couldn't be more rotten, I must tell you that the reason there were two cribs in grandmother Teschner's bedroom at 37 Thaxter Road in Newton, Massachusetts is because one is for me and the other for my grandmother's fifth son, Allan, born a few months after me. (That's right. I have an uncle younger than I am!)

There's more! My younger brother, Douglas Paul, aka "Skippy", deceased in 1992, at age 52 – "multiple organ failure" – gangrene – He simply gave up trying to find someone to replace his lost mother -- suicide of a most morbid kind -- looks nothing like either my sister or me. With wavy light brown hair, skin tone, and facial features-- he looks exactly like his five uncles, suggesting he is, as many suspect, grandfather Teschner's son – not my brother, not my half-brother, but my ¾ brother, begging the question: Did incest cause my mother's abandonment of me -- getting as far away from Newton, Massachusetts -- west to Yakima, Washington as possible?

My mother's father – not uncle -- grandfather Teschner is really my grandfather – I'm his first-born grandson, but he never shows it. I never remember him even talking to me. I'm afraid of him. He's first generation German.\

The first thing I would see inside the Teschner's house fat 37 Thaxter Rd. in Newton ,is a glass case full of trophies grandfather Teschner won at Harvard and a big photo of him winning a race against a guy with a big "Y" on his shirt

My father's equal part in this nefarious nuptial begins with similar sexual shenanigans, to wit, he is also a bastard born to unmarried parents. However, unlike being called "Brother" and held incognito for three years until his parents married, my father's mother secreted her infamy by donating the fruit of her wanton womb to an orphanage in the Allston section of Boston.

While visiting his counterfeit Coleman relatives at a wedding across the street from 37 Thaxter Road, my shy, insecure, rejected father is seduced by 16 or 17 year-old "Sister Janet" – my mother.

Ed and Pauline Teschner, whether or not they knew of my father's attempts to find his biological mother, are nevertheless wary of any male marking "Sister Janet's" pedigree tree, and twice deny my father's request to marry "Sister Janet."

My parents elope to New York in June-- taking me along for the ride, *in utero*. I'm born the following January. Do the math.

Had the Justice of the Peace asked me -- perspicacious pre-person that I was, if I opposed the marriage I would have answered; "Hell yes! The groom, orphaned at birth, denied his mother's milk and his adoptive mother's love, and the bride, denied her rightful parents and likely being the mother of her father's son, this marriage's chances of surviving are less than a turtle with two broken legs making it across a LA Freeway during rush hour!"

Some 20 years after my father's death in 1987,while going through his papers not claimed by my half brother, I discover a small envelope containing my father's Birth Certificate, listing him as Richard Otis, not Richard Coleman, son of James T. Otis, mother/s maiden name-- Mary A. Curtis—married name -- Inez

May Otis, of the famous Boston Brahmin Otis blood line, including James Otis, Sr., Attorney General of the Massachusetts Bay Province, Mercy Otis Warren, writer and considered the "Conscience of the American Revolution," Samuel Allyne Otis, First Secretary of the United States, Harrison Gray Otis, third Mayor of Boston and president of the Massachusetts Senate, a later Harrison Otis, publisher of the *Los Angeles Times*, Elisha Otis, founder of Otis Elevator Co., and Amelia Earhart, to name a few.

For 60 years I'd been ashamed of my family, not having any real relatives, therefore rootless – belonging to no one and no one belonging to me – always the outsider in a group which belonged to each other , but not to me.

My father died in a nursing home at age 74, from the last of several strokes, having had MS for 40 years, and prostate cancer – going full circle from orphanage to nursing home, never knowing that instead of being orphaned without roots, his was from Otis blood bluer than Atlantic his ancestors crossed in 1633.

My birth certificate lists the address of my parents as being 205 Oakland Street, Wellesley Hills, Massachusetts, my mother's age as 17, my father's 22, and his job, "clerk'– (grocery store ?).

I recall many images of my crib years and terrible two's., Once, while playing ball circa age two, in the street, BAM! I get hit in the head with a baseball which is why I couldn't say "linoleum" or "aluminum' until my second year of graduate school, jump rope, get arms and legs working together so as to fake being a fish, or do trigonometry.

Just before, or just after that incident, my mother jerks me up by one arm, and hauls me into our kitchen, where she rams a bar of Ivory soap into my mouth for saying a word I could only have heard my father utter, swearing being his only extraordinary talent.

My sister may have been born just before we moved from the bungalow in Dedham to Dunedin Place in Wellesley.

… I do remember men hanging around the kitchen at Dunedin Place – the milk man, the Cushman bread man, who ran over my football, the ice man cometh --methinks too often and stayeth too long, and the landlord, whose German name was changed to "Mr. "Wissle" to accommodate my baby brother's limited linguistic repertoire which did not include "Wechsler".

That I observe my mother inviting this attention while my father is working gives me probable cause to distrust and dislike her.

I'm even expelled for a day from kindergarten with Jack Malone for fighting, certainly warranting consideration by the Guinness Book of Records .as the youngest kids ever expelled from school.

One day, Jack Malone, and I are sitting on the stone walkway leading from the road up to the front porch. We are honing our skills as nascent, if not naughty -- certainly nefarious-- stone cutters, or in the alternative, displacing our anger on hapless stones.

My sister, considered by both Jack and I to be among the most terrible of the "Terrible Twos," sticks her nose – literally– between a shard of wayward stone, which, if not intercepted by my sister's intrusive forehead, will fall without fanfare on the ground. Instead, it gives cause to shrieks not heard since *Jeanne d'Arc's* torching, trailing my sister as she flees through the neighborhood in search of our wanderlust mother, who, with unforeseen punctuality pounces on me like a lioness, jerks me up by one arm, and disallowing either of my feet to touch the ground, launches me into the upstairs bedroom, where, still holding me suspended in space, begins whipping me with her ironing cord. (The paper thin pants of my Royal Canadian Mounted Police uniform offer no protection against her lashes, nor the marks left behind on my behind..Yet, I will not cry. Not until she dumps me on the floor, and I hear her close the front door, do I indulge myself in tears of pain and her rage reciprocated.

… Once a criminal always a criminal. I next perpetrate an act of treachery against my baby brother, resulting in dire consequences intended for him, but in fact, a life sentence for me.

So it was after lunch our mother makes us take a nap – sister Carol age two, me a just turned four on our mother's bed, with baby brother Skippy, not yet walking, in his crib.

After being certain my sister is asleep and our mother is downstairs, I slip out of bed, lift my baby brother over the railing and out of his crib, set him on the floor, and slide back in bed, feigning sleep.

To my chagrin, "mommy dearest," upon finding her infant son on the floor, absent any signs of "foul play" – to wit, the side rail of the crib is still up, concludes her youngest offspring is her *wunderkinder* – her little genius. She so proselytizes this family myth, that instead of getting baby brother in trouble, I unwittingly get him anointed "the brains of the family."

So, word goes forth throughout the land, (*Boston Globe?* Probably not), that baby brother is a genius a reputation he will take to his untimely death at age 52 – having gotten no closer to genius than dropping out of Tufts University, and his reputation as being "the brains of the family" unchallenged by my Ph.D.

On an early fall afternoon, walking home from school alone, after crossing the bridge over Route 9,and climbing the back stairs to our second story flat, an event occurs which both changes my life forever, and scars my psyche for the same length of time.

Upon locating my mother in her bedroom standing next to her headboard -- my sister and baby brother peeking through the footboard, my eyes track to an adult male in my father's bed, a sheet up to his chin, and his navy officer's cap on the nightstand.

"He's sick and I'm taking care of him," my mother claims.

She's lying. I'm four years old, but I know she's lying.

I'm not clear on the timing, but soon thereafter, I'm deposited at a foster home – a scary, cold, old, brick, two-story, mini-mansion on the corner of the trolley line between somewhere and Coolidge Corner in that part of Boston, called Brookline. With all the downstairs curtains pulled -- the dark living room, to a frightened four year-old, smells and feels like a place that doesn't cater to kids, at least not live ones.

The only time my father visits me at the foster home is to take me to his adoptive parents – Nana and Pam Coleman's – I think for Thanksgiving

….I'm riding shotgun in his black four-door Nash – more like standing or kneeling beside him, He begins sobbing – looking like he can't see the road. I put my arms around his neck, telling him, "Everything's going to be ok. Everything's going to be ok!'

' That's what I said. What I believed was we was that we're heading toward a telephone pole -- He's not turning the wheel. We're going to crash, I jerk the steering wheel to the right, sending the car careening up on the sidewalk and lawn, but missing the telephone pole.

With his head on the steering wheel my father is sobbing uncontrollably. I rub his back as I repeat, "Everything's going to be ok,"

I felt it then and I believe it now; my father intended to kill us both.

Sometime later I go to court in Dedham. Nana and Pam Coleman, and I think my father – as always in the background – like the waiter at the *Last Supper* – also in the court. I'm told to sit on the chair near the judge, who is looking down at me. The judge asks me if I want to live with Nana and Pam – not my real grandparents, but my adoptive grandparents,

I say, "Fuck no, Judge! I want to go back to that dark, seemingly haunted house, run by a loveless middle-aged man, himself seemingly haunted by the death or disappearance of his wife, in which the *Lord the Flies,* rules these unruly wards of the State of Massachusetts!

Just kidding. I did go to live with my father's adoptive parents, "Nana' and "Pam. Coleman.

My adoptive grandmother is Jeanette Coleman, maiden name, Boson of the Boston French Huguenot Bosons of newspaper publishing and banking interests, who, grandmother Coleman, aka "Nana" bemoans, "My father lost his fortune in the crash of the 1880's."

Pam, of the Newington, New Hampshire Colemans, tells me he enlisted as a teen in the Spanish American War, dreamed of becoming an architect, and designed and built the house at 980 Greendale Avenue - old Route 128 – in Needham, for a reported $5,000. (Nana sold the house after Pam died around 1963-4. for $16,000. In the 1980's and 90's it was worth $250,000, and within the past three years, the house was torn down and replaced with a house priced at ONE MILLION, THREE HUNFRED THOUSAND DOLLARS!

During my years ages 6-10, Pam was my Geppetto –bespectacled, Falstaffian-girded, jolly maker of whistles out of tree branches, carver of weather vanes, reciter of *The Jabberwocky,* and Civil War devotee, who never raised his voice, cussed, scolded, nor bore false witness against his neighbor, or relatives, and who asked nothing of life but good food in large quantities.

I was his Pinocchio, wanting so much to be his real boy, all of which embittered my father, who now resents both his father, Pam, and me, his son.

Only once did the three generations of male Colemans recreate together. We attended a Boston Red Sox game. I was eight or nine. We sat between third base and the Green Monster, Joe Cronin was the shortstop. Ted Williams was being trained as a fighter pilot.

The day after he retired, he took up permanent residency in his favorite living room chair beside the front window, and until going to the VA hospital in Dedham to die, that's where he dosed 24/7.

On the day before he died, I saw that he had shrunken to a skeleton of his former self – maybe 120 pounds -- prostate cancer among his killers. Standing there in his white hospital garb – as if in a witness lineup of the walking dead – he emitted an odor I had never smelled before or since. I reflexively thought, "He'll be dead tomorrow." He was.

If my father's relationship with his adoptive father bordered on censored civility, his relationship with his adoptive mother, "Nana," as far back as I can remember, was a war of mutual resentment: Nana was not the mother he had hoped to find, and he was not the son she hoped to adopt. Both constantly reminded each other of their reciprocal grievance by their mutual avoidance.

I became the weapon each used against the other – I became Nana's favorite to spite my father, and my father's son, so he could take me back from Nana, when in truth, neither wanted me.

So, I lived with my father ages birth to 4, Nana, ages 5-10, my father, age 10-15, then back to Nana, ages 15-19 -- my father had thrown me out. (By the time I'm

18, Nana and Pam are too old to cope with a teen five decades since they were teens and a teen not even their real grandson.)

When I first went to live with Nana, at age five, my bedroom is upstairs in a small room previously used for storage, but now space for an Army cot and my cloth covered toy box. I don't recall a dresser but there must have been one. I remember playing alone for hours in the bedroom with my metal "army guys." one in a white uniform on skis, with his gun strapped to his back. (Nana's Rule: All toys must be put back in the toy box regardless of the stage of the battle.)

It was in that room when one night, having trouble falling asleep or having awakened, upon thinking about God and church, I thought. 'One day I'll write my own Bible.' I didn't of course. (By age 16, I was a closet non-theist. Some 80 years later, I did write, "God: The Greatest Lie Ever Told – The Torah and Bible for Smart and Funny People Only,"

In winters, my cot is moved into the second upstairs bedroom, sometimes occupied by my father. Clothes hung in a small closet enclosed by a gray cloth curtain hung on a rod. On those nights I was alone, I feared falling asleep lest Nana would come out of that closet and kill me.

She never did. I never even caught her trying.

I also never saw her smile, and certainly not laugh There were just too many "thou-shall-nots" requiring her vigilance – too many temptations to be guarded against, and too many bowel movements to monitor – hers and those of other family members -- publically.

Any physical signs of affection – hugging and kissing is wrapped in a warped sense of sex, the former to be avoided lest it slip into the latter.

However, the only sin which concerns me is that

none of the adults – not my father, not Nana and not Pam, offer me an explanation as to why I'm not living with my mother, why my mother left,, when will she come back, what did I do to make my mother not want me anymore, and what did I do that is so bad, to get me sent to that scary foster home.

.   At age five and beyond, my story translates, "I've got to be sure I don't do anything wrong so I won't get sent back to the foster home. At age nine, "I've got to be the best at everything I do if there's any chance of being loved." At age 16, "My own mother rejected me; females not my mom, will certainly do the same." At age 22, "Maybe if I marry someone young she'll not see the fatal flaws in me that my mother saw, (wife #1). At age 42, "No woman will ever love me so I must 'over-love" her," (wife #2). "If never love, at least sex," (wife #3), and at 56, "Irony of Ironies, my mother is finally found – in truth a cloned Borderline Personality incapable of loving or being loved – our son as expendable to her when he was four as I had been to my mother at age four.

I remember feeling, but not thinking, that the mother's love I lost could be won from my peers by being the best at everything I did -- baseball, football, hockey, kick ball, and most importantly the best at "Russian Shmuck." -- my recess favorite in which one player scoops up the loose football, and must then weave his way through all the other players on route to the goal line without being "shmucked" -- tackled.

One first such pursuit of the admiration of my peers -- had my foot misstepped a few inches, would have ended me.

I'm five. Nana sends me to the "Little Red Store" about a mile away for a loaf of bread – Wonder Bread, of course, and a dime to pay for it.(I now pay $4 dollars for a loaf of bread, while genuflecting to the

Gods of capitalism;)

Barbara Holden, a year older and her brother David, a year younger, walk with me. (Maybe I offer a popsicle as an inducement.)

Two houses above Nana's is a bridge over the train tracks running from Needham Heights to Boston. An adult's waist-high concrete barrier on both sides of the two-lane highway (Old Route 128) discourages drivers from plunging to their certain death.

The distance to the tracks below is more than the distance to the clouds on a rainy day, but less than the distance of the prop planes flying overhead to and from Logan. (Recalculated as an adult, the fall would seem to be 30 to 40 feet.)

On the return trip, with the loaf of Wonder Bread clenched under one arm, I may have asked, Barbara and David, "Dare me to walk across the top of the railing?" or more likely to thwart a "No" response, I hop up on top of the 12 -inch wide concrete rail, slanted down at each edge, to begin my improvised tightrope walk spanning some 40 feet across.

My need for their approval trumps my fear of death, while incurring Nana's disapproval -- Her scrunched loaf of bread victim of my fear, trumps her concern for my safety.

I'm sent to my room and Barbara and David are sent home.

I cannot remember Nana ever punishing me before or after. (Pam was not the only one on Nana's short leash.)

At age six, I take a girl friend -- for one day. (Actually, she "took" me, as I am about to explain.)

The distempered temptress's name is Evelyn Gilliland. She's in my first grade class. She's six..

Just as Freud predicted, during the last days of my Phallic Stage, and a few days before I would have found sanctuary in my Latency years, she suddenly and unexpectedly intrudes into my life. In truth, she ambushes me as follows:

First, I distrust anyone who wears a dress – a dress can't keep your legs warm as can be plainly seen and dresses are totally useless in protecting against scrapes, scratches, bruises, and cuts while playing "Russian Schmuck." And girls are so nosey and noisy – yelling and screaming at recess. And their hair – always combing, brushing, twirling – a boy caught with a comb is a "sissy" or worse.

Anyway, she invites me to her house, which is about three football fields from the school. After taking me inside to meet her mom – maybe we have a snack – we then go outside

Like awkward honeymooners on their first night, we stand around on the sidewalk not knowing what to do or say. She, perhaps immobilized between wanting to play hopscotch, yet attend to her mother's admonition to be a "good hostess" -- Me, thinking wrestling somehow seems logistically unworkable. (She's still dressed in her school dress and probably doesn't know how to wrestle anyway.) Guessing she doesn't have a bat or ball and not sure "hide & seek" or "red light/green light" will work with only two people, we shift from one foot to the other, start to say something, only to stop mid-sentence.

When her two playmates from across the street join us, the awkward tension becomes palpable.

Suddenly, absent any known provocation, Evelyn slaps my face hard, Smack! My cheek stings. My ear rings. My heart cries..

I try to hide my tears by sliding behind the telephone pole made convenient by its proximity. But the telephone pole's sanctuary fails – insufficient in timeliness and girth.

Trauma thrice suffered – once by the sting of the slap, second the humiliation of being brought to tears by a girl, and last and most hurtful – rejection again by a female I had dared to want,

I walk home. It's only about a mile. I was supposed to call Pam to come get me.

Forever more, Evelyn Gilliland's rejection without probable cause would be added to the list of rejecters begun by my mother.

I peak in the fifth grade, not surprisingly, my last year of childhood and the year before puberty will change all the rules of engagement.,

"Aunty Dot" – my father's adoptive older sister and Nana & Pam's only biological child, lives at the top of Byrd's Hill up behind Harris Elementary School! When the wind is from the west or not blowing at all, she reports hearing boy's yelling, "Coleman! Coleman!" trying to persuade me to pick them for my baseball team at recess.

I'm the most popular kid in the school – even Miss Lane's fifth grade favorite – why else would I win the Best Penmanship Award and "King of May" for the May Day celebration which included dancing around a real maypole? (Actually, I had my tonsils removed so my reign as King was shorter than Pippin IV's.)

I was the only one who could kick the ball up on the school roof, hit a ball into the yard next to the school, and score the most touchdowns in Russian Shmuck.

The girls and Miss Lane seemed to think I was cute, which I discounted as being irrelevant to athletic prowess, and therefore gratuitous, meaningless, and bothersome, as was my nickname "Handsome."

At a Saturday matinee at the downtown theater, arranged and scripted, of course, by girls in my fifth grade class, I'm assigned to sit next to Judy Curran, who the girls decree is my girlfriend – my discontent with my consent ignored. By ways of communication, known only to them, they surreptitiously float – promote -- the plan that at some time during the movie, I must consummate this affair by holding Judy's hand.

I reluctantly submit to participating in such a public scandal only after promising myself to exercise the option of jerking my hand away immediately upon feeling hers flinch or recoil. Stalling as long as I could, and, as if putting my hand on a hot stove, I slide, my hand on top of Judy's, thereby eliciting gasps from my classmates racing left and right up and down the row of theater seats, with faces leaning forward to confirm the incident for posterity.(Hey, the year is 1946, before, *Playboy*, before the sexual revolution, and before porn.)

Experiencing no pain, I leave my hand copulating on hers until my sweating palm exposes my trepidation.

I had no premonition at the time that 1946 would be the best of times and the worst of times -- The best of times because, Ted Williams, returning from World War II, becomes my hero, idol, role model, and surrogate father by default and proxy. The Red Sox win the American League Pennant. The Needham High Hockey team wins the Bay State League and Massachusetts State Title by beating Lexington 5-0. (Andy Faye, a neighborhood dad takes us to all the Needham hockey games and three of the Red Sox games. At one of the Sox games, we are at the hot dog stand when Ted hits a home run! Geez, I plan my summer, so to be near a radio in the first, third, sixth, and ninth innings, or when Ted was expected to come to bat. A hot dog more important than seeing Ted hit a home run. Blasphemy! Off with the kid's head who demanded a hot dog!

But most all, my fifth grade classmates at Harris Elementary School like me -- I'm popular. I feel I belong – they are my family. None of the kids care, or even know, why I don't live with my parents, that these aren't my real grandparents, about my mother abandoning me, the foster home, or about my sister or brother. (I'm as ashamed of me and of my family as Ted Williams was ashamed of his, and like Ted's teammates, my classmates don't know I'm ashamed.)

I win more medals at summer camp than any other camper – Beginners, Middlers, or Seniors. I'm the youngest player on the camp's baseball team, the flag football, and rifle team, and should have won "Best Camper,"-- older kids are congratulating me before we even go inside for the banquet.

Instead, I lose to a "did nothing kid," who didn't win a single medal or play on any of the camp's teams.

I feel a banquet barn full of kids looking at me to see my reaction when the other kid is announced as the Best Camper of all the Middlers. If they expected tears, they were disappointed. (My mother "taught" me not to cry.). This kid was even a non-entity in my cabin of 10 kids. I was later told that his father was a generous funder of the Camp Director's (Reverend Pratt) church -- my first introduction to "dirty" politics – "it isn't what you know, but who you know."

The best of times becomes the worst of times on that Labor Day weekend. Nana, Pam, and I visit my father in Hollis, New Hampshire, where he is now living with his new wife of a year ago, their son of four months, and my sister, brother, from their foster home, where they had been for the past four years.

As I get ready to leave to go back to Needham with Nana and Pam, without warning or discussion, Nana aside whispers, "Your father says you're staying."

Shocked. Stunned. Numb -- Without a culprit to attack and predisposed to turn inward, I run into the only bathroom and lock the door, where I stay until the well of tears runs dry.

When my step-mother convinces me others need access to the bathroom, I move grief's emergency room to the woods behind the house from where I plot to walk back to Needham as soon as the others are asleep.

Hollis is a small town of some 1,000 farmers, where everybody knows everybody -- not a place where I can hide my past. Everyone will know about my mother, about the foster home – about the divorce …My step-mother says this house was once a one-room school – All I know is that it's dirty, smells bad, too old, too small for three adults three kids, and one baby – another house to be ashamed of – kike ted was ashamed of his …water is hand-pumped at the kitchen sink or carried in buckets from a spring in the woods from across the street. Later, another bedroom is added to the end of the house and in-house water faucets take the place of the hand pump.

My step-mother is home taking care of my six-month-old half-brother -- more like my one-quarter brother.. My father losses his job at the mill in Pepperell, Massachusetts, because he's got multiple sclerosis. My step-mother's shell-shocked brother, (Anzio beach) feeds us from the final days of a once prosperous farm – now down to 8 cows, a few chickens, fewer ducks, an old horse, tractor, and an apple orchard yielding only a shrunken harvest of brown insect infested apples.

My step-mother, ex-home economics teacher, earns a little money by sewing clothes. My father , soon diagnosed with MS works part-time as the only telephone operator in town, before slurred speech ends that job, He becomes wheelchair bound, unemployable, bitter, brittle, ill-tempered, the little pride he ever had decimated, his new wife and her live-in shell-shocked brother, targets of his "slings and arrows" – his verbal tirades against this most recent outrageous misfortune..

As regular as the ocean's tide, \he routinely makes hurtful statements to my step--mother to cause her to cry, which in turn, turns me into the family's marriage counselor at ages 11, 12, 13, 14, and 15, offering my step-mother a shoulder to cry on -- literally -- more reasons to hate my father for treating her so badly.

The reality is that who else would have married my father – an emotionally scarred factory-working husband with three kids, all of whom show early signs of being "basket cases?"… Ok, the other realty is that my step-mother – I could never use the word "mother" back then and even hesitate now – she's 32, single, and midway on the "plain Jane – ugly continuum.

The Hollis school grades 1-12 are taught by one teacher going back and forth between two classes in the same room, for example, my sixth grade class sits on one side and the fifth graders on the other. (One could argue a 12th grader has the equivalence of a six grade education, n'est pas?)

Six grade teacher Miss Deneaux (sp?) is cruel, verbally abusive, sadistic, and political – picking on the poor kids and sucking up to the ones from money. For example, one day, after handing me a broom and telling me to sweep the floor, referring to me, she snarls, "What's the matter city boy, no one taught you how to use a broom,"

. On another occasion, she slanders me before both classes. "No one wants to play with a cheater," referring to my valid claim that I (poor kid) was safe at third because David Wright (money kid) dropped the ball.

Looking back, I learned nothing grades 6-9, cannot recall a single book I read, and other than a few most common words in French I, would have learned more if I'd been raised by wolves.

In the seventh grade I started as a forward on the high school basketball team, second-baseman/outfielder on the high school baseball team and in the 9th grade, I'm captain of the first ever high school football team – ok-six-man flag football, but a first-ever football team none the less -- me barely 5'7" and 140 pounds. I was also the youngest player on the Milford American Legion baseball team playing against teams from Nashua, Manchester, and Concord. .

A soon as I move to Hollis, my step-mother, arranges for me to have a girlfriend. (In retrospect, other kids and adults were always trying to play matchmaker, independent of any request by me for their intervention – Geez, girls scare me. I don't understand them, They don't play sports. They wear dresses, which make no sense and they scream all the time! They're from a different planet!)

In the 8th grade, a person or persons unknown, place a Kotex in my locker, which I simply discard as waste paper. My step-mother, having been subsequently hired as the home Ec teacher, explains to the school principal that I must be forgiven for I knew not a Kotex was,, could not have brought Kotex to school, and therefore must not be punished for I knew not what I had had done.

Our closest neighbor on the Nashua end of Pine Hill Road, through woods to a pedophile's house, was 18 year-old Bobby Nartoff, who took advantage of my 10 year old innocence and naiveté, by hugging and kissing me on our walks home from school.

My father, too caught up in his own problems, never considered that I was being tutored by a nascent pedophile.

That next summer, between 6th and 7th grade, I'm indentured by my father, without my knowledge or consent, to my step-mother's crippled Uncle George. I leave each morning at 5:30 to get a ride with my step-mother's older brother who works as a machinist in Chelmsford, Massachusetts, and is a man of no words.

My job includes loading and stacking wood for the kitchen cook stove, cutting hay, loading hay onto the tractor-drawn trailer, unloading the hay up into the barn's loft, cleaning the cow stalls – shoveling cow shit – maintaining the large vegetable garden, mowing the yard with a push mower, and whatever other jobs needed doing. I work from 7:00 AM until being picked up by "Uncle Jim" – no real uncle of mine, around 5:30 five days a week from mid-June through to the end of August. (I know I was working there on August 16, because that's when it came on the radio that Babe Ruth died.)

It wasn't until October or November that Uncle George spays me via a Government Bond worth $18.00.,or six friggin' dollars a month, $1.40 a week , or $ .28 cents a day, or .$.03 cents an hour!

Once again, my feckless father betrayed me – didn't have the guts to talk to me first -- Had to go behind my back. I'm his son, for Christsake, not his fucking slave. Just like sending me to the foster home! Just like making me leave Needham! Another reason to hate him as if I needed any more reasons.

Decades later, I ascertained that the winter before I was sent to live with my father and step-mother in Hollis, he, my step-mother, and my sister and brother, stayed with Uncle George and Aunt Kay, while their present house was being made livable – It never was -- my father had sold his eleven year old son into involuntary servitude to repay Uncle George, in part, for letting my father and family stay with them that winter!

Behind the unscreened and unglassed back porch, which became my year r-round bedroom – snow on my bed on winter mornings -- the land inclines about six feet, putting an old rusted oil barrel at eye level from my bed on the unscreened and unglassed porch. (Someone had used the barrel for target practice for it is pock-marked with large caliber shot-gun pellets,

I would eye the barrel from my bed designing a way I could stand in front of the barrel and pull a string to fire a gun from the porch. Other times I would try to will my heart to stop beating. (Neither worked as you can clearly deduce. Is there more reason to castigate and self-flagellate than to fail suicide!)

I don't belong in Hollis. They're about farms, while I've got Boston, not bulls, in my blood -- Ted Williams, the Red Sox, Celtics, Bruins, the Boston Pops, Arthur Fielder, Harvard, the Cabots and the Lodges – English snobbery and exclusiveness – The American Revolution, Lexington and Concord, the *Boston Globe*. Bill Russell, Bob Cousy, Red Auerbach's cigars, Cape Cod, baked beans, brown bread, and hotdogs Saturday night suppers, Nantasket, codfish, the Charles River, Cardinal Cushing's Hail Mary cants on the radio, AND, I had no idea back then, that I had Boston Brahmins in my blood line. I'm an Otis, but find out too late -- 50 years. too late (I could be related to Elizabeth Warren!)

I must to go back to Needham before I get so far behind in school, I'll never catch up!

I've been buying my own clothes and providing my own spending money since the 7th[h] grade, working summers on Hardy's Farm picking beans strawberries, and hoeing corn, haying, cleaning hen houses, riding shotgun for egg runs to South Boston, weeding gardens, shoveling snow, roofing houses– It seems I'm always working for someone - not counting all the free labor done at home and for relatives, hauling and splitting wood, hauling water from the brook up to the barn for the cows, cutting hay with the horse, putting hay in the barn, painting the room added to the house…

Meanwhile, my father pays not a dime for my support during the years I live in Hollis -- 1946 until the fall of 1951. In fact, my father paid nothing toward my support since he and my mother split when I was four years old.

We live on Pine Hill Road – maybe a mile or two from school and seemingly uphill both ways. I save $60 dollars working the last summer of my discontent at Hardy's Farm, and buy a motor bike -- a bike with a small motor attached

"From ancient grudges breaks a new mutiny" - - no Laertes and Polonius here – My father goes ballistic, verbally attacking me for buying the motor bike, for spending $60 dollars, for not asking him first, and orders me to take the bike back – he isn't going to let me ride it.

This from a father who never talked to me about why my mother left, why she never came back, why she never sent me a birthday or Christmas card -- about how she died – why we didn't go to her funeral – (He does make it known I must never mention her name, which has a way of interdicting my questions), never talked to me about putting me in the foster home, why he never came to see me … never asked if I wanted to leave Needham, Nana and Pam, my friends and the only security I had ever known, albeit with grandparents who weren't really my grandparents, schools he had himself attended and were reported to be among the best public schools in Massachusetts, never talked to me about moving to Hollis, working as a indentured servant for Uncle George – no uncle of mine-- for three months at six dollars a month, never talks to me about girls, sex, how to pitch, bat, tie my tie, about foreskin, never warns me that Bobby Nartoff is a homosexual predator, never talks to me about God, or why I have to sit through the preacher's tedious, trifling, trite sermons, when he himself didn't even go to church!

We had never argued before. Like my mother, he didn't talk to his children – certainly not his oldest son, so there could be nothing about which to argue. His petty hatreds were sprinkled like pepper throughout his salty expletives and "Goddamns." He hated Jews,("Kikes"), Catholics,("fish-eaters"), Cardinal Cushing, Dublin Irish, ("Micks") -- mistakenly thought himself to be Northern Irish, -- intellectuals, (Ph.D.'s bull shit "piled higher and deeper") and Italians ("Guineas") He hated my step-mother's live-in brother – the tension in the house keeping everyone on edge.

By hyphenating his petty peeves with "Goddamns," I inferred no room for discussion or challenge existed.

We are enemies, not father and son He believed Nana and I had conspired against him. Asserting the role of father –come-lately – too lately -- forcing me to leave Nana and Needham and come to Hollis, was his way of getting even. – Oedipus Complex, of a most profane, perverted, and unkind kind.

The confrontation ends, when he commands – with words I may have provoked, "Get out and don't come back … Call Nana. Maybe she'll take you. You're not staying here!"

I did. She said, "Yes."   '

"Yey!! I'm going back to Needham and my friends!'

But Nana & Pam are older now and their muted reception stills my excitement.

I must repeat French I, algebra I, and be placed in a low geometry class. My home room and algebra teacher "Asa" Small, my biology teacher "Bugsy

Gates," American history teacher Jack Frost, English teacher Miss "sleeping pill" Steel and PE instructor Phil Claxton all taught my father, who had told me stories about each one. As none of the stories, except those about Principal Mr. Pollard, depicted a positive relationship, I pray my father was a forgettable student. He wasn't.

Needham Junior High fields teams in football, basketball, and maybe baseball, meaning I will be at least at a four- year disadvantage in all sports, particularly football. So for example, the first day of practice, I must watch other players to learn how to put on the shoulder pads, do the calisthenics, and run plays. Nevertheless, I was one of only two sophomores on the starting team – defensive back – 5'8" weighing 147 pounds, striking fear into the heart of any 195-pound full back daring to venture into my zone. (Not exactly. Our own 195-pound fullback Don Riley, in a practice scrimmage, ran over me like an 18-wheeler over a caterpillar, leaving cleat marks on my inner thigh which still exist.

Asking a girl for a date would be like asking Episcopal Reverend Hall for advice about masturbation.

Never having seen a naked female-- *Playboy's* first edition Marilyn Monroe copy didn't t ignite the sexual revolution until 1953, the year before I graduate from high school -- I know nothing about the female body parts, or how they work.

My only sexual experience was once being jerked off in the back seat of a car on the way back from the beach. I'd known how that body part worked since I was 12., My only question being how did she know?

It just made it that much worse when females knew so much more than I did! (As a four year old, I thought Nana wore those funny shoes with big heels because that's the way a woman's foot is shaped. Don't laugh --True story.)

More importantly, I'm missing some basic definitions. What is a woman? Why is she so emotional? Why do her moods change so quickly and so often? If she seems to like you one day, she may act like she hates you the next? Why does she cry so easily What is a "period" other that a dot on a piece of paper? How are babies made? And above all, how do I get a girl to love me when I couldn't get my mother to?

Mr. Ferret, aka, "Black John" -- high school English teacher extraordinaire – career maker/breaker -- without an "A" in his senior English class, you can tear up your application to one of the Ivies, West Point or Annapolis.

He instantly installs me as one of his favorites, nicknames me "Curly," places me front row -- middle desk, right under his nose and has me raking his eaves, mowing his lawn, etc.

I'm flattered. At last I'll be able to shed the label "Jock" – not "dumb Jock" but not Ivy League Jock" either – At last, someone who recognizes I have a brain.

"Black John" is, of course, not black, There is not a single Africa-American in Needham, and few, if any in the surrounding towns, so I infer "black" denotes the "executioner" role he plays in the lives of competitive high school seniors desperate to use Harvard and Yale as the springboard to the good life..

"Black John" is 6'1"or two, 230+ pounds,, mid 50's, with shoulders of an NFL linebacker, a Beethovenesque head, wavy salt and pepper hair, and a glass eye. He wears a bow tie and tweed brown suits right out of a Thomas Hardy novel, has a booming basso voice, chain-smokes Camels, sometimes leaving tell-tale patches of cigarette paper on his lip and is just as addicted to coffee.

During an English class he falsely accuses me of plagiarizing a paper I had written, without any specifics and in front of the whole class. Not only is the accusation false, but it is out of character – he would have talked to me, or any student, after class, or in his office. I'm confused, hurt, feeling betrayed, and distrustful. Why did he falsely accuse me and humiliate in front of my classmates while pretending to be my father?

Black John acquires a New Hampshire get-away, and asks me to help him dig an outhouse, During a break for milk and cookies he announces unprovoked and irrelevant to our conversation, "You're one of us," repeats it, and when I look puzzled, repeats, "You're one of us," rises and goes into the kitchen.

The following summer, while helping to build a stonewall at a new house he has built, he asks me to drive him uptown to buy a pack of cigarettes. On the way back, he points to a dirt path going into some woods, "Pull in here, I have to take a leak,:

I did. He did. He wants to talk. It's mid- summer. We're hauling and lifting stones. I'm wearing a t-shirt and shorts back when shorts were short.

Suddenly, his large, heavy, hot hand finds its way high onto my bare inside thigh.

I snap my leg away, flip on the ignition, ram my car into reverse, careen backward down the path, my vision too blurred to keep on my tire tracks, without tree branches scratching the car, sounding like a finger nail across a chalkboard.

In stoned silence I deliver Black John to his house, stare straight ahead waiting to hear his car door shut. Then I drive down to the river to shed tears of anger and betrayal – betrayed again by an adult representing himself to me as a parent, grandparent or surrogate.

Decades later, as a psychologist, I realize that shaming me – getting the victim to commit some act of wrongdoing "softens" – makes the young trusting victim vulnerable for sexual exploitation – the altar boy drinks wine, the neighbor's kid looks at *Playboy* or *Hustler* or watches porn with the pedophile, or Black John falsely accuses me – shames me – in front of the class – for an act of plagiarism.

When he insisted, "You're one of us," that day I helped him dig the hole for his outhouse, he was trying to persuade me that I'm a homosexual like him and Dr. Brody.

I forgot to mention Dr, Brody – repressed the memory. By way of making home visits to care for Pam, Dr. Brody becomes our family's doctor

I'm unsure as to the specifics, but at some point I ask him if he can give me anything to help me grow – I find no comfort in the statistic that 5'8.75, in 1954, is at the bottom of the average range, nor the observation that the majority of my male peers are about the same height. Dr. Brody invites me to his office (in his home) implying that help is an office visit away. I go two or three times and each time Dr. Brody injects a clear fluid into my shoulder. (Probably water. as I stayed 5'8.75).

There is something about Dr. Brody which makes me uncomfortable -- his slippery smile – as if he were flirting -- sneaky -- as if he were doing something he shouldn't, or wanting to do something he shouldn't. Anyway, he is a doctor -- Harvard Medical School. His daughter is a classmate – the least attractive of the females. Maybe he's just trying to be extra nice to me so that I would date his daughter.

Some time later, I visit his office, perhaps for a routine physical exam for football. He asks me where I'm going to college, I say I don't know. (There is no way I can afford college – Nana and Pam make no overtures to help, even though Nana had received $16,000 from her brother's will. ($143,600 in 2017) Besides, I'm not their real grandson.

Harvard educated paternal grandfather Ed Teschner and school teacher Pauline Teschner refuse to admit I'm their first-born grandson – in their view- son of "Sister Janet" and therefore, not their grandson – and worse – a reminder of their "dirty secret."

I cannot call it "interest," but Colby College in Waterville, Maine, invites me to visit. They lose the football game 50-0. I see a future of prolonged hospitalization from playing quarterback at Colby, if the offer were to be made. It wasn't.

Dr. Brody offers, "I can get you into Harvard Medical School, \but first you must learn to give a massage," he promises as he strips down to his jocky shorts and hops, face up, onto his treatment table.

With all do speed, I exit his office, never to return.

With no other options, I commute to Boston University for a year, which seems more like going to work at a factory in a big city..

I need to go away. The older I get, the more I feel unwanted – the game of pretending I have equal standing with the rest of the Coleman clan is over. My father has expelled me from Hollis. My mother's family – the Teschner's never admitted I was one of them.. It didn't help my claim to a place at the end of the Teschner''s table that my mother is dead.\

I want to live on a campus. I want to go to an Ivy, specifically, Brown University – Harvard for the middle class, or so I thought. I need money. I get a job working 2nd shift and "graveyard" for American Can Company packing paraffin orange juice cartons and then as 3rd shift janitor. During the day, I deliver newspapers, paint houses, and whatever jobs I can find.

I save $1,500, which is the equivalent of $13,238 in 2016, and apply to Brown University where one or two of my mother's brothers had attended. One went to Dartmouth, and I never knew where the oldest went

I take the SAT's. The Brown interviewer leaves the room. A glance at my SAT results looks like my score is 753 out of perfect score of 800 – (I had not taken any chemistry or advanced math in high school).Brown encourages me to apply, so I do.

Mid-August I call Brown to inquire as to the status of my application. "You're application was placed on the inactive list because we never received your transcript from Boston University."

"But I have the receipt right here from BU for the money I paid for the transcript!"

"I'm sorry, but the deadline period for applications is closed,"

Due to the encouragement from Brown, I had not applied anywhere else, Had I worked three jobs and scrimped for a year for nothing? So it seemed.

A week or so later, Black John calls. Nana tells Black John that Brown turned me down, which wasn't what happened, but Nana painted with one brush – the black one.

I make hand motions signaling I don't want to talk to him. After she hangs up, she lectures me for being ungrateful for all the help he had given me – even trying to get me into Harvard, which was never going to happen. (I've heard Nana's lecture on gratitude and being "thankful" all my life.)

Black John calls back a few days later. (There is no caller ID in 1956.) I answer. He's talking as if his planting his large hand high on the inside of my thigh never happened.

He says a former student of his at Braintree High School married a psychology professor from Duke, who will see about getting me into Duke.

I check; Duke's tuition is $3.400. Besides, other than a trip to Quantico Marine Base to visit Joddy's much older and married sister, I've never been south of Providence, Rhode Island.

It is now early September. Classes are imminent. Black John calls. He tells Nana to put me on a train for Greensboro, North Carolina. His professor friend will get me in somewhere.

So Joddy's father and mother, along with Nana and maybe Pam, drive me to South Station in Boston where I pay for my ticket – no one offers to help. I feel as if they are telling me "good riddance"- and board the train, accompanied by all my worldly possessions packed in one of Pam's World War I trunks

After traveling all night, I arrive in Greensboro, NC before dawn,

The dark, dank station belches a hundred smells – all foul. A sign on the cinder block wall reads: COLORED. I look around – All that I see is hues of gray – gray cement walls – gray doors – gray trains— gray railroad cars – gray steam – a few brown faces, but nothing "colored".

When the African-American taxi driver, asks, "Where to?" I answer, "Greensboro College"

The driver, looking at me in his rear view mirror, says questioningly," That's a school for young ladies."

"No! That's not possible," I exclaim as I reach into my pants pocket for the information and the professor's phone number, reasoning, "Greensboro College must be where Dr. Hornaday teaches, not where I'm going.... 'I know Black John wanted me as far away as he could so I wouldn't blow the whistle – tell the world he's really a pedophile. Even so, he wouldn't be so mean as to allow his professor friend send me to a girl's school! Would he? Or did he care as long as he got me out of Needham?'

The men's dorm is an old two-story brick house on the corner lot across the street from the campus and the Administration Building.

A few males are hanging around. They don't seem any more pleased to see me than I am pleased to see them -- instant mutual dislike.—a north/south thing. Apparently the word on the street is that a damn Yankee is invading -- enrolling and that must be me.

After parking my trunk at the foot of my bed, I flee downtown to shed tears of despair on the insouciant sidewalks of downtown Greensboro, North Carolina.

'I'm out of here on the next train to DC. I'm not going to a frigging girl's school! How would I ever tell my friends! Damn you Black John! Damn you!''

Somehow Dr. Hornaday finds me walking the streets with my head down. Too late for me to wipe tears from my face, he motions me into his car and drives me back to campus and a meeting with the college president – an Orrin Hatch/ Mike Pence polished face, smug in the delusion, that they alone have a direct line to their god

The foster home and Hollis revisited --once again forced to live as a stranger among the unwelcoming. Twice my father and now Black John throw me under the bus -- rather put me on the bus to hell.

' … A college for girls! I don't even like girls – I don't trust them – I'll cross the street if I see two or more walking toward me…Christ! Now I'm going to be surrounded by hundreds of them! Suppose my friends find out. Nana must never know -- I can't ever go home now…, I'm out of here. I'll go to the t… But, I've already paid the tuition – "Damn you, Black John! Damn you!"

The year, before, Greensboro College, formerly a debutante "finishing school" for rich Methodist daddies to prepare their daughters to marry the son of a another rich Methodist daddy, began accepting males, but only commuters.

The first day of Miss Stinson's French class – I'm the only male -- Geez, I feel like a male stripper at convent vespers.

The bell rings. As I'm figuring how to extricate myself from the classroom as unobtrusively as possible, from the back of the room comes a voice, as sonorous as a harp. I turn with the same amount of deliberation as my knee straightens whenever tapped with a hammer by my doctor.

I trace the voice to one the three girls huddling – to the one who seems to glow. Never before have I beheld beauty's perfection – Carolina blue eyes – cupid's lips – round cheeks seeming to be as soft as a baby's bottom .She blushes, or has she drawn heat fresh from my flush. The other two girls twitter,

Suddenly aware that all the girl's and perhaps Miss Stinson – are watching me staring with my mouth open and my face afire, I scurry out the door stalked by giggles' echo.

Research in the literary yearbook yields her name to be Doris Cloninger -- Miss Charlotte in 1954. She's a Junior Maid of Honor, from Paw Creek.

'Geez, even her home town sounds magical.'

I next see her waitressing in the family style dining hall, She's a music major who frequents the O'Dell Music Building next to my dorm – converted old house.

My only non-essential possession is a small $30 portable record player and a few records brought from home. When alone in my dorm room and the rest of the residents in class, Mario Lanza and I sing Don Jose's *Flower Song* and other operatic love songs to Doris.

We sit facing each other in Mr. Flaccus' (sp?) 8-10 student American Literature class. I try not to keep looking at her and consider myself more self-disciplined than most – never had a lighted cigarette in my mouth , never consumed a beer, nor any alcohol, yet even with the threat of incurring her displeasure, I cannot stop stalking her Carolina blue eyes …She is not 15 feet away, yet separated by my 20 years of insecurity

Doris does "not go gently into that good night." Almost 40 years later, during the development of a novel's love scene, she emerges from the tenuous obscurity of my subconscious into the role of my beloved Lori in my novel *The Governor's Fingerprints*/

Fifty years and four wives later, indulging in the fantasy that my last words from death's bed will be "Doris" not *Citizen Kans's* "Rosebud," I indulge myself in the promise I will see Doris one time before death's interruption. After several months, I call her.

I can't believe she remembers me.!Her husband died a few years earlier. She lives alone in a townhouse in Charlotte.

We exchange phone calls. I think she may have even initiated one or two. She agrees to see me and even seems enthusiastic/ During one or more calls, she posits the absurd hypothesis that I will be disappointed.

The date is set. I'm getting a second chance after 50 years.

On the plane, "I'm as giddy as a toddler on a swing, I haven't seen a crocus or a rosebud,' but it's the first of April and an early spring.

I rent a car. Her address is maddening difficult to find. Trembling like a teenager on his first date. I knock. She opens her door --Beauty lingers in her blue eyes and on her gentle cheeks like a September sunset at the beach.

We reminisce about our college days and exchange histories all day and into the night. Normally reticent – guarding against exposing my vulnerability to love's confession – I am now ebullient, spontaneous and fluent.

It now seems too much so.

One of her daughters joins us, I get the uneasy feeling she is checking on me. The next morning one of her son–in–laws calls to see if Doris is ok – a ruse implying my visit is malicious -- itself an act of malice – for never was a lover's mission more pure in its intent.

That morning – we slept in separate bedrooms of course -- while holding her in my arms for the first time, I say the words I did not deserve to utter 50 years ago. "I love you, Doris," and kiss her, also Mission Impossible in 1956.

For her part, she plays her piano and sings, but unhappy with both results, stops with a flustered apology.

I worry, 'Why does she think she needs to win my love, when my love for her was won 50 years ago? Has my coming here not reassured her?.

This is not as I had planned –fantasized-- and her daughter's pre-emptive visit and son-in-law's phone calls have cast the specter of suspicion on my visit so to salvage and protect a love that had survived 50 years, I plan to leave on an earlier flight back to New Hampshire, during which I promise myself to move to Charlotte to begin anew that which I left unfinished in 1956.

Back in New Hampshire, I call Doris before even taking off my coat. No answer. Perhaps she's asleep. Same result the next morning – afternoon-- day – next day -- next three days. Desperate letters are unanswered.

First, I blame her family's suspicions as to my motive, then a bad background check, (to be explained later) then Doris being angry with me for waiting too late.

I send a birthday card with flowers and the next year a Valentine card with flowers, Her phone number is changed to an unlisted number.

Acute depression and sadness both become chronic. I must have an answer before death's interdiction …'Hop a plane to Charlotte? No, I don't want Doris to refuse to open the door, or worse, see it's me and slam the door -- rejection more cruel than my mother's!'

…Back to 1957. I'm sitting at a table in the college library. A girl's hand drops a one inch piece of orange crayon, tied in a bow by a piece of string, in front of me and walks away. I follow first with my eyes and then ,as if repeating the primal scene of Eve's hypothetical seduction of Adam depicted in the fictitious Garden of Eden.

She leads me upstairs to a room filled with student's painting -- some on the wall, some on easels. She shows me hers.

She introduces herself Jane McGregor, from Gibson, North Carolina, the only child of Mason and Frieda McColl McGregor, short, blond, blue eyes, cute, art major, trying to move beyond Gibson and the "petty pace" she so derides -- a rebel with a cause

As the person being pursued, I'm awash in cognitive dissonance – absent the fear of rejection, but uncomfortable in this foreign juxtaposition of gender's liturgy.

Our time together increases exponentially, as a train descending the mountain absent its engineer and we as its only passengers.

It's a Saturday afternoon .The antebellum brick

Greensboro College Administration Building is open, but empty and unlighted. She appears to know where to go. The room is dark – drapes drawn. ..

We begin kissing. She submits her nipples to the fretful feast. Her hand takes mine where it has never been – She guides my tremulous tumescent penis into her hot slippery vagina, then impatiently she grabs my buttocks to power my hard thrusts into her.

Absent all cerebral protocol, I'm operating as my ancestors did after they realized they had to come down from the tree to mate.

I'm unaware as to when and how this first foray into sex ended. I do remember she starts crying as if I'm the reason for her tears.

'How could that be when she lead and I followed?' I ask, with no answer forthcoming.

Later alone that evening I ask myself how she knew the building could be entered, how did she know that it would be empty, who was the source of the information, had she been there before, with whom, and under what circumstances?' Doubting Thomas's absence is always so very brief'.

Undisturbed by the lack of answers I, the follower now becomes possessive -- jealous -- not willing to share her with even her roommate, causing me to wonder, 'Is male possession of his mate always the outcome of sex's initial gig?

Her subsequent behavior is dominated by making said body parts available to me on a daily basis.. Meanwhile, she transfers from Greensboro College around the corner to Woman's College, now called the University of North Carolina in Greensboro), moving our moveable sex feast to her new dorm's "study room," between library stacks, at night on the campus golf course, and frequently in my red 47 Plymouth convertible brought down from home. One time she even smuggles me into her dorm room while her roommate sleeps. (Famine, so soon to gluttony turns)

In retrospect, motivated more by fear of losing her than by love for her, on the railroad tracks running beside the campus, assured by Jane she will say "yes," I ask her to marry me -- her choice of place to propose, not mine. She usually sought to do the unusual, or the do the traditional at a most unusual place.

The cost to control her – possess her -- keep her from leaving me is a $500 dollar emerald cut engagement ring, worth $4,300.00 in 2017, which forces me to sleep in my car that summer and eat one meal a day consisting of a hot dog "all the way" and a small soft vanilla ice cream cone, while I work as a playground supervisor/baseball coach for the City of Greensboro, to make my monthly ring payments.

On her dare, I pose nude (jock strap) for her art class, buy her a skirt with the $8 dollars I earn, but begin realizing I'm working too hard indulging Jane at the level I established a year and a half ago. The ring payments are taking a toll, too. I have to sell my convertible for the same version of a beat up coupe. So is maintaining her daily diet of sex taking time from my studies.

Finger fucking is the *modus operandi*. The usual place -- an unlocked study/visitor's room in her dorm. (Pulling her skirt down is far less a problem than pulling my pants up.) Yes, the romance, if it ever existed, becomes ritual sex, where the excitement is not getting caught which trumps coitus in general and *coitus interruptus* in particular..

I begin reviewing the relationship without realizing I'm beginning the end. To justify my retreat, I revisit the past -- recalling one day while she is still at Greensboro College, I happen by her classroom door, She's copying answers to a test from the girl sitting next to her! During a visit to her home in Gibson, I'm present when she accepts $100 from her mother contingent upon her stopping smoking. I'm also present when she later tells her mother she's stopped smoking. She hadn't.

If she lies to her own mother, why wouldn't she lie to me? Besides, who taught her so much about sex? She has no sisters and certainly not from her deeply religious Methodist mother … Had she cried that first time to make me think she's a virgin?

I tell her I need time to think, which is a half-truth at best. I need a rest. I'm worn out trying to control her – prevent her from leaving me by servicing her every whim and want.(It never occurred to me, that she may have been sacrificing her body to control me.)

Meanwhile, Dr. Hornaday, the psychology professor "Black John" contacted to get me out of Needham and into a college – my unofficial mentor, comes to the dorm around noon to tell me I've been expelled from Greensboro College and must leave immediately.

By that second fall, male students arrive from Ohio, Florida, and western North Carolina, but there is still no PE and no gym for the male students, half of whom are genotypic males, one is a flaming giggling queen, three appear to have been neutered, and one is running around with his umbilical cord still attached. We have to recruit teens in the neighborhood to have enough for flag football in the yard beside the dorm.

One night we decide – I may have made the suggestion – to carry a music professor's VW Beetle from its parking place on the road by the Administration Building to the fountain in front of the Administration. implying, not too subtly, his car needed washing.

At the end of that second year fall semester, the convent of about four or five wimps – wusses -- one

guy/girl,, and two Southern Baptist wannabe preachers,
must have complained about the out-of-state rowdies –
especially that damn Yankee from "Massatuessets."
because the spring semester brought us a :house mother.

I couldn't believe it. A goddamn housemother!
What was that phony, eunuch Reverend Whatshisname
College President thinking?

I'm expelled, I guess as the ring leader. I make
no such claim, or more likely, as the only Yankee from
the liberal state of "Massatusetts".

In addition, that last semester, I had taken a
night shift job at P. Lorillard Tobacco Company as a
hopper boy – using both hands to lift loose tobacco out
of a canvas tub and placing it into the cigarette machine.
After two weeks, both arms break out into a fire-red
rash, and I could no longer breathe through my nose.

At the same time, I'm taking a required Religion
course. (I distrust all occasions in which the words
"required" and "religion" appear in the same sentence.)
The course meets at 8 o'clock. I guess any later and too
many students would fall asleep. Well, I'd worked the
night shift so I'd fall asleep anyway. One time I ended in
the front row. When I wake to the bell ending class, the
professor of Religion – Christianity – the Methodist
version – the professor's vision of that version, glares at
me. The girls twitter.

The College President is a free-lancing
Methodist minister. I'm certain he and the Religion
professor discuss this unruly Yankee factory worker,
falling asleep in a Religion class – blasphemy -- the
same recalcitrant Yankee who had also, during his first
week on campus, led a non-violent "sit-out" protest
against mandatory Methodist chapel service every
Thursday forenoon.

This Northerner, outside agitator, trouble maker,
non-believer contaminating Greensboro College's

virginal co-eds must go.

This is 1957.. This is North Carolina. This is Jim Crow country, where oppressing African-Americans is the state's *raison d'etre* So, why was I shocked that Greensboro College expelled me – an honor student-- without anything in writing, no warning, no hearing, no grievance opportunity, no probable cause, and no due process? I wasn't surprised. I was shocked as to the process..

Once my draft board finds out I'm no longer in college, they will have Korean War on their minds, meaning I have in mind some redneck sergeant from Mississippi ordering me to scrub toilets with a toothbrush 'on account he doesn't like Yankees in general and those from "Massatuessets" in particular, "so I shove said toothbrush so far up his ass he can brush his teeth from the inside, and for so doing, I get court-martialed – not an ending – his, or mine, I covet.

I sell my car and hurry down the road to Elon College because they are on the quarter system.

I'll be damned. My roommate is another Southern Baptist wuss with his Bible under his pillow.

Grandmother Teschner, who had never sent me a birthday or Christmas card in my life, sends me $20, which is $20 more than any other family member or relative ever sent me.

My Personnel Psychology instructor, a real intellectual lightweight with an alleged Master's Degree from Harvard, professes that capitalists are not in the business of making money, but rather simply to make products. I must have somehow indicated I believed he was full of shit, because he gave me a "B" (I got "A's" in my philosophy and English classes, and despite being out of baseball four years since high school I'm "red-shirt" on the Elon baseball team. (Why "red-shirt" a transfer from a college which didn't have a baseball team?) We go to the NAIA World Series at Sol Ross College in west Texas

I ask Elon for financial aid based on my grades and having made the baseball team as a walk-on.

Without blinking, the financial aid officer replies, "We only give scholarships to students studying to become Christian preachers."

After the thought of grabbing him by his tie and hanging him on the first tree limb I can find on campus fails reality's test, I remind him that every member of the baseball team including one utility infielder are on full scholarship, storm out of his office, slam the door, and mutter words, not printable even in 2018.

With suitcase in hand and thumb of the other begging a ride, I hitchhike back to Greensboro, where I notice the Boston Red Sox have a farm team. I begin going to the stadium while the players are warming up. They invite me to join them. One player, Bill Monbouquette, who the next year would begin his career pitching for the Red Sox, knows Mark Wenham, my classmate and friend at Needham High.

One day, the manager asks me to go to third base, where I had never played and after fielding some ground balls said something about Red Sox third baseman Frank Malzone, which I assumed was a compliment.

When the players go to the dugout for a meeting, I did one of the dumbest things in my life rife with life-changing fuck-ups. The 12 year-old bat boy motions me to grab a bat so he could pitch to me. Reflexively, I did as ordered and proceeded to miss every pitch he threw, picked up my glove, walked off the field and never went back – my dream of playing for Red Sox DOA – self-inflicted disaster -- too dumb to stop and think that I'd been hitting against college pitching, and would, of course, be way out on front of a 12 year-old's pitches.(I never saw an outfielder other than Willie Mays make catches I couldn't make, and I had a strong accurate arm. Nick Pond, the head sports broadcaster for WRAL-TV in Raleigh told the station owner I was the best outfielder he'd ever seen. I once got a standing ovation for a catch I'd made, and was surprised by the ovation, because I'd made many better, I remember a softball game – I went flat out to catch a ball hit to ,my right, and did the same to the next batter going to my left.

The problem had always been getting down on myself – a missed pitch was total failure. The best hitters are out 70 percent of the time. My insecurity and striving to be the best would never survive a 70% failure rate. Besides, with no one in my corner helping, supporting, and encouraging me during the inevitable bad games, a batting slump would be fatal …

In the last game I played for a "touring" softball team, the pitcher walked the hot-shot hitter young enough to be my son, to get at me. I was moving back to Massachusetts and this would my last at bat in my last game, I hit a grand slam home run. The manager said, "Just like Ted Williams." I beamed.

For $2 dollars a night, one can get a cot, pillow and blanket in the basement of the Greensboro YMCA. I soon learn that by sneaking in, covering my face and feigning sleep, I could avoid detection by the night watchman's flashlight ferreting for freeloaders.

Guilford College has a downtown campus. I enroll in a math class in trigonometry, the terms of which makes no sense. What in hell is a "sine" or "co-sine"? Is this course a conspiracy of willful and malicious obfuscation??

I plead my case to the retired math instructor, "I'm educationally challenged – only the left side of my brain works. I did get hit in the head with a baseball when I was two – 50/50 chance my right side – my mother also had a Rocky Marciano right hand."`

There is, of course no God, but that merciful math instructor comes close by giving me a gratuitous "Gentleman's "C".

I now get a job at a Franklin Drug Store, as stock boy at $1.00 an hour, enroll full-time at Guilford College as a psychology major after concluding: (a) There is no future for a philosopher in a capitalistic society, (b) An English major predicts a life as a starving writer, and I've done enough starving, thank you very much, and (c) Maybe psychology will provide answers to questions about my mother I'm unaware I'm asking, such as, 'Why did she abandon me at that foster home, never to be seen or heard from again"

I attend classes until noon, work at the drug store from noon until noon, work until 8 o'clock, then return to widow Teague's boarding house where I rent a bedroom with kitchen privileges for $15 a week.

My senior year at Guilford, a Mr. Vance arrives as the second member of the Psychology Dept. -- the other being the Dept Chair, Master's level psychologist, and wife of the College President. (I believe it's called "nepotism")

Mr. Vance is not a psychologist, but rather an admitted Master's Degree/ Divinity student from Boston University, who decides to go into missionary work of a perverted kind – not to convert the uninitiated to Methodist dogma, but rather to rid the world of all disciples of the atheist Freud, who in the 50's, upon information and belief, held sway at Boston University.

The first day of my class in physiological psychology, Vance, whose experience and training in physiological psychology was suspect, begins by asking, "Is anyone here Freudian?"

I smell a rat – Vance -- and avoid the trap. Tragically for me, a female student from Paris France, who I thought liked me, pointed at me and says, "He is."

The trap snaps shut -- on my neck.

I'm also auditing a pre-med class in physiology.. Vance doesn't know the difference between the properties of a cell and the functions of a cell, or at least thinks I don't know, he doesn't know and, based on his ignorance, grades my answer "C" and "C" on my first test.

I learned early (kindergarten) to never question a teacher's pedantry, and that said rule becomes increasingly rigid as one moves from elementary to college, so that by the time "teacher" becomes "professor," one's grade depends on total capitulation to the vanities, prejudices, and predilections, of the professor.

Refusing to suspect that Vance would be so corrupt as to perpetrate whatever treachery necessary to make certain this Freudian undergraduate student never gets into graduate school, and despite the above-noted warnings, I make an exception in Vance's case by presenting both textbooks to Vance showing Vance asked for properties of a cell, but graded me on functions of a cell,

Big mistake, first by Vance and then by me. Vance gets defensive, refuses to consult either textbook, and refuses to change my grade.

It gets worse – much worse. Vance willfully and maliciously continues his corrupt grading practices on the mid-term by crediting me with a "C" for "A" work.

It's no longer a game. Vance is sabotaging my career and doing so with the apparent blessing of the head of the Psychology Dept./wife of the College President, both devout Quaker . (Guilford is run by, of, and for Quakers, who are presumably only slightly less anti-atheist Freud than vicar Vance.

Back then, I preferred to think there is no collusion, but a fellow student, who I thought less capable, but who embraced the Quaker *Weltanschauung* and indulged the College President's wife in her conceits and vanities – she once boasted she read a book a day – I was unimpressed -- went on to distinguish himself as an MMPI authority and editor of an abnormal psychology textbook..

Desperate situations demand solutions in kind. I do something I've never done before or since. I cheat.

Vance's final exam comprises five of eight possible questions. I pick my five. The one Vance poses as a "gotcha" question, namely, the "point to point" relationship of rods to cones in the human eye according to French scientist Lorente de No, I write word for word from the textbook. I didn't have to, but I can't take chances with Vance. Graduate school and my career in psychology hang in the balance,

Vance still gives me a "C" on the final exam, "C" for the course, and "C" on a lab, thereby, aided and abetted by the College President's wife, sabotaging my chances of getting into graduate school and a career in psychology just as he (they) intended to do.

Hire a lawyer to sue Vance, the College President's wife and Guilford? I'm making $1 dollar an hour as a drug store stock boy!

In 1960, college students in North Carolina had no rights. In 1960 North Carolina, Billy Graham and Jesse Helms are in, Sigmund Freud and Charles Darwin are out. Furthermore, it doesn't seem to trouble or dissuade Vance, or the Chair of the Psychology Department/College President's wife that I simultaneously take an "Honors" class in Theories of Personality that same semester in which I'm orally examined by an outside psychologist in front of all the other psychology students, for which I earn an "A," or that I am the top psychology student, and an "A" student overall , who despite the two "C's" from Vance graduated 24th.in his class.

In retrospect, I didn't respect the Head of the one person Psychology Department – two when Vance was added -- graduate of the elitist Wellesley College, with only a Master's Degree -- no real intellect, a dilettante, who was Department Head only because her husband is the College President. I didn't respect her and she resented me. (Another mother problem?).

If it looks like collusion, sounds like collusion, and smells like collusion, it's collusion. (Persecuted Quakers, persecute non-theists, persecuted Jews persecute Palestinians, persecuted Christian persecute Jews, etc., etc., etc.)

It would be another six years before I earn a Master's Degree and another three to get my Ph.D.

Ironically, seeing psychoanalysis irrelevant to the male incarcerated delinquents I was being paid by the State of Massachusetts to "cure," and equally irrelevant to school and institutional behavioral problems, I eventually became Skinnerian, after al..

One afternoon, I notice a middle age woman walk into the drugstore with her teen-age daughter leading the way as if a poodle on a leash. I've seen them in the store many times before, but this day I think, 'Pity the poor slob who gets involved in that situation.'

Some time later, the pharmacist approaches me just before I go off the clock and, handing me a prescription envelope, says, "The customer wants you to deliver this on your way home. Her apartment is right across from Greensboro High school."

I'm as puzzled by his expression as I am by the mission. The drug store has a father and son delivery service. Why me? Why this customer?

I knock on the apartment door. A scratchy female smoker's voice yells, "Get the door."

The door opens by a seemingly embarrassed and blushing teen, effortlessly attractive, long black hair, large brown eyes, seductive in her innocence.

"Well, just don't leave him standing there! Invite him in," the smoker's voice commands, its source coming forward from a room, presumably the bedroom at the back of the apartment."Get him some pie and ice cream"

The mother, hereafter referred to as "Mrs. Robinson," close-up accepting the prescription from me, is as sketchy as she sounds scratchy -- layers of war paint – lipstick making lips where none exist, eyelashes like needles – mascara leaking – falsies which would make Dolly Parton envious, and mid- brown hair bristled by being over cooked by a curling iron.

Over the next year and a half, pie and ice cream move down menu, replaced by home cooked steak and baked potato suppers, free tickets to Greensboro Generals hockey games in the new Greensboro Coliseum, built in no small measure by her boss and former mayor of Greensboro, Bill Sullivan, Sr., tickets to the Greater Greensboro Open, and an Elvis Concert, where a yelling and screaming menopausal Mrs. Robinson, with a red bow in her hair out-teens the teenagers, while her daughter and I slink down in our seats, trips to the beach, and tickets to the movies for her daughter and me.

The following summer, her daughter suddenly notifies me with a confused and apologetic look, that that they will be going to the beach for a week. I'm not invited. (I have to work anyway, but I'm still hurt and confused..)

I spend the week sanding and finishing the living room floor, replacing the carpet, and painting and cleaning the entire apartment.

I'm sitting on the front steps when I see their car arrives, and head up the walk to meet them anticipating how pleased and surprised they will be when they see their refurbished apartment.

"Mrs. .Robinson," emerges first, walks right by me without so much as eye contact. Her daughter follows shrugging her shoulders as puzzled as I by her mother's rudeness. Third in line, I watch Mrs. Robinson unlock her front door, enter her apartment, and disappear into their bedroom (Mother and daughter sleep in the same bed and daughter never uses pronoun "I" but always :we". I remind myself of that afternoon over a year ago, when upon seeing Mrs. Robinson with daughter on leash, parade into Franklin Drug. "Pity the poor slob who gets involved in that situation."

I leave. Later that evening, a Greensboro police officer serves me with an arrest warrant for stalking "Mrs. .Robinson," and ordering me to appear for a Hearing.

At the Hearing in the basement of some random downtown building, I encounter a middle-aged male dressed in a suit sitting at a desk – a State of North Carolina flag on one side and US flag in the other, one or two lawyers or plain clothes law enforcement people, Mrs. Robinson's boss, and company President Bill Sullivan Jr., haunts the background like a preacher at a Saturday night supper /fund raiser. Mrs. Robinson glares bullets

It has the look, feel, and smell of a staged Jim Crow hearing, but in any case, if the purpose is to intimidate me, it works.

Mrs., Robinson testifies that I stalked her down her walkway as she tried to get away from me and continued to do so by forcing my way into her apartment.

I'm issued a Restraining Order forbidding me from being within a certain distance of her and her daughter's residence and the mother's place of business.

In return I'm offered no chance to defend myself, no attorney, and no opportunity to question my accuser.

Wronged by another woman – another goddamn mother! Southern Jim Crow injustice. Another example of southern payback against a damn Yankee!

This mother's egregious injustice must be avenged!

Surprisingly, her incensed daughter turns on her mother, suggesting we run away, adding, "We'll have to get married."

"What better way to avenge Mrs. Robinson's treachery? I ask?

We flee to Myrtle Beach in my 1952 Chevrolet, are married by a justice of the peace, and then re-enter North Carolina on our perilous flight to Massachusetts, with one eye on the road ahead and the other tracking the road behind in the rear-view mirror.

Nana's first question to me in a hastily arranged private inquest is, "Did you get her pregnant?' (The sting implied, "Like your father did to your mother?")

Without revealing how hurt I am with the question, I simply answer, "No, of course not,"

Soon, a Needham police officer knocks on the door and orders us into his patrol car based on a call from "Mrs. Robinson," (No warrant, no notice of the charges, or even if there were any charges, and no right to violate our Fourth Amendment protections against unlawful seizure of our person.

At the police station, the officer tells us to wait. Maybe 15 minutes later, a Catholic priest arrives, who intimidates, berates, and threatens my teen bride that if she doesn't annul the marriage, (to a non-Catholic), she will be ex-communicated, and sent to hell upon the event of her death.

Catholicism in the raw – A rare glance into the role of the Catholic priest -- to hell (literally) with a confused, frightened, and conflicted teen age parishioner who might -- sin of sins -- marry a Protestant and raise their children, Protestant – lost revenue to the Catholic Churches' coffers. (The Vatican didn't become the richest per capita country in the world without exploiting their poor parishioners.

And what of the Needham cop who misused and abused his role as a town employee to function as a *de facto* representative of the Catholic Church? He was fired, right! No? The Chief was probably Catholic, too,

.For my part, I soon discover that revenge is like aspartame – sweet for so ever brief a time, but long in its bitter aftertaste

After 12 years and two daughters, Wife #1 looks elsewhere for the father I was not, finding him in the married Mormon father of four living across the street, who, just being neighborly, warms my bed when I'm consulting out of town

Accepting the bias that girls need their mothers more than their fathers -- our two daughters born in a home divided – the older daughter mine, the younger hers, I move into an apartment.

In hindsight, had I been a better husband, -- including, rather than excluding, my wife in my life, there would have been no Mormon interloper.… Many years later – so many years too late, I wish I could make it right, but I can't…If the Mormon were to die, I would ask – beg her for a second chance, knowing the chances are slimmer than none …Recall, Johnny Carson and Ted had similar sentiments for their first wives..)

Around the time we separate, (1974-5?), I become the clinical director of an alleged drug treatment program at Duke University Medical Center, where I become entangled with Meg, a co-worker and daughter of a Duke professor.

The highlight of that triste encounter is an all-night sex excess. When we awake the next morning, she purrs, "You're amazing – seven times!"

The low point is when Meg abandons me at the Hiatt Hotel in Atlanta for her drug dealer in Murphy, NC, which is where I somehow find her after hitchhiking for eight hours from Atlanta to Murphy. (Days or weeks later she shows up at the clinic, I ignore her.)

Enter Pam Roberts, my former administrative assistant, when I was the Director of NEPIC – Nationwide Educational Programs in Corrections, a 22 – state consortium of state agencies dealing with delinquents,. She's back in town needing a place to stay and a job.

An ex- Duke graduate, Pam married a Duke med student, who, she subsequently ascertains is homosexual, divorces him, and when I last met her, is living with a hippie in Shaker Heights, Ohio.

She now tells me she's been accepted at the University of Southern California Film School in the fall and needs a job in the meantime.

I tell her she can stay in my apartment while she's looking for a place and that one of my staff (Meg) has quit, and that I'll try to get her into Meg's spot. (Do you see the parallel to Johnny Carson - the compulsion to always be involved with a woman?)

I have a one bedroom apartment, so I sleep on the sofa in the living room. I had yet fallen asleep that first night when I see Pam standing close enough for me to feel her naked body heat.

"I'm horny she says," walking slowly back to the bedroom.

I follow. We copulate during which, anticipating my timed *coitus interruptus*, she says, "I can't get pregnant."

Well, yes you can, and yes you did – that night – the very first time!

Without seeking my feelings, she aborts. I had always been attracted to her. I want her to have the baby, but she is more ambitious than she is motherly. She intends to become one of the first American modern female film directors – no time for marriage, babies, or husbands – with one exception -- a Sugar Daddy – me..

I get her the job. Sometime later, I and my staff, concur that the clinic is misrepresenting its public solicitation that people will receive treatment for their drug addiction. In truth, no treatment is provided. The clinic is a "front" for lead research psychiatrist Dr. Ellinwood, to develop and copyright, at NIDA's expense, a computer diagnostic system to identify classes of drug abusers and addicts, focusing on amphetamine abusers.

We call Ellinwood's hand. He fires all of us except his research assistant—a Ph, D. psychologist and the computer programmer.

I'm offered the Head of the School Psychology Department at Western Carolina University – I'd been previously told I could have a professorship at Chapel Hill, but I would have to undergo a sex change operation as all current faculty are males. Diversity requires a female

Although a trouble-maker, prone to act on its own, and often unruly, my penis stays – the Carolina professorship goes, as does the job at Western Carolina University -- Pam has Los Angeles on her mind, not Cullowhee, North Carolina.

Meanwhile, I too apply, and am accepted to USC Film School. (as a screenwriter). I expect Pam to be pleased. She is not. (I wonder why not.)

We settle in a two bedroom apartment, a block from the Santa- Monica Strand over-looking the Pacific Ocean. The front bedroom is set aside for my oldest daughter, who I hope will come live with us.

About every night we decide – ok, Pam decides, on the foreign film we (she) wants to see. We (she) merely scan the *LA Times* to find where it's playing.

On weekends I'm acting in one of her several student films. (No Cecil B. DeMille production here.)

I miss my daughters. The oldest is my sweetheart. I envision Duke-educated Pam becoming her step-mom.

One Sunday, while lunching on the Strand, I broach the plan of bringing both my daughters to Disneyland.

Pam asks, "Can we afford it?" (Her question implies; "No we can't," and more directly, "I need the money for film school.")

I'm stung. She knows how much I miss my daughters. She knows I'm bankrolling the move to LA, and her living expenses. (Realty check: She has no interest in me beyond my role as her "Sugar Daddy.).

The Pam Dream ends. I've fucked up again! I leave all the furniture – everything –- my heart – my dreams – my MG – everything except my books and fruit of the looms, and pulling a U-Haul trailer, drive someone else's car back to Raleigh, where I'm offered temporary housing by a woman counselor working for one of the state agencies, for which I had done psychological evaluations. She s a single parent of two teenagers.

On the second or third night I'm awakened by her trying to put into effect joint occupancy of my bed. I defeat her effort and move that morning,

I purchase a modest brick house in the Raleigh Little Theater District, set on the side of a hill.

One Saturday afternoon, I go to the door, surprised to find Anne, a former Raleigh debutante, formerly married to a prominent Raleigh attorney and now married to an architect.

As I'm looking around her in search of her car she explains, "I rode my bicycle so my husband couldn't follow me. I want you to fuck me."

The conundrum of having women make the first move just to avoid them rejecting me as my mother had done is having to reject those making the first move Being hypersensitive to my own pain from being rejected, I can't be insensitive to their pain, can I? No, of course not! Anyway, Anne is married. To that add the fact that Anne's round hard face, dark hair, strong build, promiscuous manner, and aggressiveness regurgitate images of my mother.

My awkward effort to rebuff Anne as kindly as I could – actually my empathy must have sounded to her as equivocation, in turn encouraging her to be more assertive. She had been a frequent acquaintance, but not yet a friend.. She leaves, slamming the door. My mother would have done the same.

I was twice saddened – once for having disappointed her and secondly by hurting her feelings.

A secretary in the same office as the one writing my psychological reports invites me to her house for supper, and after her two children are in bed, a "tour of her bedroom," thus beginning a suspected, but never spoken, "sex-- for-- marriage" contract lasting nearly a year.

Even for a slow-learner like me, I finally figure out this good and hard-working mom is sacrificing her body and sense of self-worth to secure a husband and father for her children. I'm using her. I hate myself for having taken advantage of her –a picture of her mother standing outside her trailer-home hit me in the face – a marriage was not in the cards, yet I still persisted with the sex-for- marriage arrangement -- She had been too good to me to continue the relationship and too good to me to hurt her by ending it.

The solution? I compound my shameless behavior toward her by taking the coward's highway – I disappear.

My testing/consulting business prospers. I sell my little brick 'shithouse" on the side of a hill, and move west to prime Raleigh real estate up above Crabtree Mall, by buying a single story house overlooking my own three acre pond – called 'lake" in the south, on 12 acres of woods, with an Olympic size heated swimming pool. Chocolate clapboard siding, pumpkin trim, and sliding glass instead of windows gives the look and feel of a Japanese whorehouse – an untenable conclusion in that I've never been to Japan and have never partaken in the pleasures offered by a whorehouse – Japanese or other.

Now, maybe at last, I have the appearance of sufficient prosperity to attract a female of my choosing. …But, have females I've chosen fared any better than those who made the first move? Let me count the ways. Tie score 0-0. Total fuck-up either way, including, a Marilyn Monroe look-alike I selectively forgot to admit -- confess to -- my only affair which lasted only two months.

So what do I do to find a woman now that I have the leverage of my newly acquired mini-estate? Hiring her is not an option as I'm a one-man operation. I don't

drink, do bars, church is against my religion, I belong to
no clubs or organizations, and avoid parties for the same
insecurity felt by Johnny and Ted. And I'm divorced –
wearing "D" as Hester Prynne wore her "A

Bingo! Rent my guest house behind the pool --
the time honored "bait and switch" used since fictitious
Eve baited an imagined Adam with an apple.

I advertise in *the Raleigh News & Observer* for a
female tenant with an art, music, or writing background.

My first choice is a purported artist. She agrees
to be vetted at her apartment. She is attractive -- blond –
Playboy type – too good to be true? Yes. Over her
mantle is a paint-by-the-numbers tiger – the kind sold on
empty parking lots along with Elvis towels.

My second choice cancels. The third choice --
call her "K," an elementary school art teacher and
graduate from ECU – no Playboy type here – but an
over-achiever well-schooled in fake seduction and
simulated southern charm – a Back Widow Spider type
too late revealed.

I offer her the guest-house rental, (In a life upon
which mistakes rain for 40 days and 40 nights every 41
days, this mistake would become a life-changer moving
in a downward spiraling maelstrom to destroy me..

While the guest house is being remodeled, "K"
occupies one of the two bedrooms and bathroom at the
other end of the house. After about the third or fourth
night, without an invitation, she slips into my bed.

I feign sleep when, in truth, her late night
partying during the week gnaws away at my already
suspect women-selection ability. This night I offer her
no reaction to her trespass. She's being vetted. Why
doesn't she know that?

The following night, again after midnight, she
ups the ante, by beginning to sob as she discloses she
has just discovered her ex-roommate and her boy friend

– a leading Raleigh drug dealer -- have been "sleeping"–
behind her back for months. (Why can't females tell it
like it is? The word is "fucking" or "fornicating." I know
of no instance in which sleeping and fucking occur
simultaneously. I offer my arm in sympathy. Luckily
she was not stopped by the cops, for I infer from her
breath, she would have flunked the sobriety test.

The next night, K skips the appetizers, the
sobbing, and foreplay and gets right into the main
course, meaning, of course, we fucked, the first of six
such moments of passion over the next six years. (As I
write this some 40 years later, in the historical context of
K earning the label of "psychopathic liar," I now suspect
she concocted the story of her roommate's and
boyfriend's betrayal for sole fraudulent purpose of using
sex to gain control of our relationship – and, post-
marriage use of withholding sex to maintain control, all
of which is confirmed six years later when, in a
sudden fit of honesty, K admits, "I marred you for your
money honey."

I cannot explain – excuse -- why, three months
later, I married K. I don't drink or do drugs, so I was
neither drunk nor stoned. I certainly didn't love her. She
was no beauty, no artist, no brain – I can only posit that
she was already living in my house, and by now, I was
no longer the head- turner I once was. I wanted a
woman – hear a woman's voice, sniff her perfumes, feel
her fundamental optimism -- to be able to see, touch,
caress, hug, kiss, and if loved, enter her body.

This introspective bullshit aside, I was
subconsciously fatally attracted to my mother's clone –
curse -- not in looks, but her personality – as it turns out
– A Borderline Personality Disorder.

Be careful what you wish for. I had wished for
my mother and found her – Hey, how was I to know at
age four my mother was a Borderline Personality? Hell,

the psychologists and psychiatrists writing DSM II,
didn't "discover" Borderlines until 1972, two years
AFTER I received my Ph.D.!

The first evening of our honeymoon – more the
first moon of a thousand night's deaths -- in a Vermont
chalet, snow a foot deep outside, with a fire in the
fireplace, K breaks the silence imposed by awkwardness
by announcing as if reading last month's obituary
column. "I've been doing cocaine for eight years..Don't
think I'm going to stop, just because I'm married."

Apparently, K's parents failed to instruct their
daughter that a honeymoon celebrates the beginning of a
relationship not its ending.

But, the honeymoon debacle is but the harbinger
of six years of a living hell – the most miserable
marriage ever a man could manage without suicide or
homicide.

As K later admitted on that day the six years of
marriage ended, "I never loved you --gag gag -- I
married you for your money honey!"

Meanwhile, the more egregious her assault on
the marriage, the more desperate my attempts to save it
– $125,000 ($320,000 un 1918) remodeling the house
inside and out – tearing down 10 tobacco barns board by
board , nail by nail, to use the heart pine to create a
"lodge ;look." quarrying stone for a waterfall sunken
shower, building a deck overlooking the lake large
enough for a medivac helicopter, vacationing to Puerto
Vallarta , weekend trips up and down east coast where
she shows her prize winning black Persian cat I bought
for her as a kitten for $750 – worth $2,200 in 2017, and
when all else fails, getting her pregnant.

All for naught. K was wedded not to me, but to
her self-interested misapprehension that "Women's
Liberation" meant she could abandon all the mores,
customs, and protocols of an American wife circa 1960

and before, while joining in the drug/endless partying *Zeitgeist* of the 1970's., all the while exploiting the benefits and perks of marrying someone – anyone – with a ?Dr," attached to his name.

For example, I don't remember K cooking me breakfast or supper, cleaning, shopping for groceries other than for her wine, beer, cigarettes, pot, and her own toiletries, never partnering in the management of the home or the marriage, not once helping in the on-going remodeling of the interior and exterior of the house, or even cleaning the pool. Instead I would return home from work to a dark, empty house, no supper fixed, no note where she'd gone or when she'd be back, or if she's be back!

Finally, I'd had enough of an empty marriage, vacant house, and deserted bed, so once when she didn't come home by 4:30 AM. I boxed and placed her clothes in the driveway for her to pick up and leave.

She did go back to Mommy – more likely to Daddy Dearest, who would now later admit his daughter is an alcoholic.

"Heaven has no rage like love to hatred turned, nor hell a fury like a woman scorned" – Congreve *The Mourning Bride* (1697). In K's warped sense of reality, the blame was mine alone for putting her things where our neighbors might have seen them.

I apologized and asked her to come home. She did, but not without reminding me of my villainy for the rest of the marriage (It lasted 6 years.)

She claimed her marriage *in absentia* was due to her taking ballet two nights a week and then partying with friends, or just partying with friends. The few times I dared inquire, she opined, , " I can come and go as I please for as long as I please, If you wanted a maid, you should have married someone old like my mother. Meanwhile I don't have to answer to you for anything I do, or who I do it with!" (I don't recall hearing those cited in her marriage vows, but I question what I was doing at the altar in the first place,.)

At the end of six years, on two successive Wednesday nights, K crawls into bed the first Wednesday night at 2:30 AM and the next Wednesday 3:15AM, both times reeking of pot and smelling like a South Boston pub. She has taken our 20 month-old daughter Shannon to two all-night pot/beer bashes and then, while DUI, driven our baby daughter home, with or without being in her car seat.

The following Sunday morning, hiding behind her *News & Observer*, she announces "I'm divorcing you. I'm taking Shannon."

During the next 24 months K takes me to court 16-18 times, including five Assault & Battery charges, four of which she is the batterer, and one, when I bumped her to get out of the baby's room, where she had provocatively blocked the bedroom door with both her arms and legs wedged into the door jams to keep me from leaving.

Another time, Judge Green, the only Wake County African-American Judge throws his arms up in disgust asserting, "This" – K's Motion over a $12 dollar prescription and to exchange interchangeable sofa cushions –"is nothing but harassment," but asks me to exchange the cushions anyway.

Accompanied by an adult female (later wife #3) who, with her two daughters waits up on the road in the car, with a cushion under each arm, I 'm waved into K's apartment (She's on the phone), and exchange the sofa cushions as Judge Green ordered.. As I start to leave, K drops her phone screaming, "Where's the rest of my stuff, mother-fucker?'" tackling me from behind and knocking me against her (my) glass coffee table causing a six-inch bleeding gash on my shin.

K charges me with assault. The Hearing is scheduled for 2 o'clock before her favorite Judge -- Russell Sherrill, who she refers to as "Rusty" and with whom she has reportedly been seen at the Raleigh Foxy Lady night club. Judge "Rusty was later convicted on drug charges.

My two witnesses and I wait for K to appear. So does Rusty. Some 15 minutes later Judge Sherrill, without calling for a recess, hops up from the bench and exits via the door behind him. A few minutes later he returns, announcing, "Kay – Mrs. Coleman's baby has an upset stomach and she doesn't have anyone to take care of the baby." and then calls the next case.

"Wait a cotton-pickin' minute," I mutter!."By making a personal call to K at her home, by acting on behalf of a party appearing before a him, and by disposing of a case as a personal favor to K, Judge Sherrill violates every judicial Canon on the books, as well as my 5th and 14th Amendment rights to due process and equal protections, and committing the felony of obstruction of justice.

"Rusty' is impeached and imprisoned, right? Wrong! This is eastern North Carolina – KKK, Jesse Helms, and Jim Crow country.

K had previously fraudulently charged me with sexually molesting my three year-old daughter,, claiming blood on the Kotex to be the "smoking gun."

The judge, her attorney, and K know the charges are fraudulent, perjured, and subornation of perjury – felonies for which all three should have been arrested and jailed.

In truth, K had failed to send enough Pamper for my weekend visitation, My female friend(later wife #3) solved the problem with a Kotex and her young daughter's underpants. (The blood was in the eye of the perjurer K).

Another time, my attorney arranges for me to get an extra day for a weekend vacation to take our daughter Shannon to Tweetsie Railroad in Boone NC. K fights my being given an extra day, but loses. When I pick up Shannon late Friday afternoon, K stages a scene in which I'm the villain taking my three year-old daughter away from her loving mother, but K NEVER mentions any problems with Shannon's foot.

We stop outside Winston-Salem for supper. When I put Shannon down on the pavement to go into the restaurant, she winces, does the same when I set her down from her highchair in the restaurant, and again at the motel.

I sleep in a chair next to her crib in the motel. The next morning the pain worsens. The trip to Tweetsie is postponed, while I take Shannon to the Emergency Room at the Boone Hospital. After an exam and x-rays, the doctor can find no signs of broken bones, insect, spider, snake bite, or other cause of the pain.

For the rest of Saturday, Sunday and Monday, I carry my daughter everywhere/ we go. (Ok, I enjoyed the closeness.)

Upon handing Shannon to her mother and explaining the results of the doctor's findings, K jerks her out of my arms, shrieking, "What has Daddy done to my baby!"

The next day K calls, "Shannon is at Rex Hospital where she may have to have her leg amputated, and 'No" the doctors won't let you see her because you are being investigated for child abuse!"

K's attorney files papers charging me with child abuse based on K's perjured statements, Again, the Wake County Judge should have prosecuted both K and her attorney for perjury and suborning perjury, making false statements to the Court, and criminal fraud.

Looking back, the evidence is: (1) K admitted taking Shannon to Pullen Park earlier that Friday afternoon, (2) K omitted telling me Shannon is experiencing pain whenever she puts weight on her foot, (3) In her court pleadings, K accuses me of causing Shannon to nearly having her leg amputated because I took Shannon to Boone instead of Rex Hospital in Raleigh, begging the question , why would I have taken Shannon to Rex Hospital when I had no notice of anything wrong until setting her down at the restaurant in Winston-Salem, two hours later. .(4) A reasonable and prudent person would conclude that K's mention of Rex Hospital suggests she not only knew of Shannon's condition, but may have caused the injury herself to sabotage the mini-vacation she so desperately opposed.

Over the next two years, on each and every visitation exchange, K creates trauma and drama for our 2-3 year-old daughter , for example by refusing to make my daughter available, telling me my daughter doesn't' want to see me, or calling the police to arrest me for exercising court-ordered visitation.

After two years of K filing some 16-18 fraudulent, malicious, spiteful, and trivial motions, all of which are without merit, after two years in which K has so alienated the affection of my daughter that I see fear in my little girls eyes every time I pick her up for visitation, and after spending over $40,00 in court and lawyer fees protecting my daughter from her mother, defending myself against K, corrupt Wake County Jim Crow lawyers, and judges, I visit the office of yet another Raleigh lawyer begging him to stop the bleeding – my daughter Shannon's and mine.

He replies, "There is nothing I, or any other North Carolina lawyer can do. Judges rule according to the maxim, 'The worst mother is still better than the best father.' This is the way it's going to be until your daughter's 18th birthday."

On December 24th 1984, we four (Shannon, later wife #3, and her 12 year-old daughter , (her oldest daughter was then living with her father) seek asylum in Canada from Shannon's evil, villainess, vindictive, and harmful mother K,, aided and abetted by corrupt , Jim Crow, Wake County Judges , by boarding a plane in Raleigh/Durham for Boston and Nova Scotia,

Shannon flourishes – happy, skipping, giggling – fear flees her eyes – love returns. Surprisingly Shannon never once mentions, inquires about, or asks for K.

When later wife #3's daughter reports that her Canadian teacher is "asking a lot of questions, alarmed, that same afternoon I meet with an attorney who tells me that as long as we don't violate Canada's laws, we have nothing to fear. Neither North Carolina nor the United States has jurisdiction in Canada.

Hours later,, while I'm reading bedtime stories to Shannon, two behemoth RCMPs, waving a piece of paper claimed to be an order for my arrest, cuff me, seize Shannon from her bed, and deliver me to the local jail.

Monday morning, I learn there will be no Hearing. The warrant was nothing but a piece of unsigned paper with the court's letterhead!

Canadian cops are as is as corrupt as North Carolina's.

With Shannon gone, there is no reason to stay in Canada. I call a friend in Raleigh who warns me that K is on WRAL-TV more than Jesse Helms and her weeping and wailing as the grieving mother has made her a *cause célèbre*, championed by Wake County District Attorney Riley, who recently lost a paternity suit, is facing charges of cocaine abuse, and whose political career is in the crapper, unless he can win back the Wake County woman's vote. Bingo! Crusading for grieving mother K offers DA Riley just such an opportunity!

Raleigh FBI Agent Pence, after first promising by phone to seek the death penalty for me under the Lindberg Law, a week or two before, suddenly recants saying if I turn myself in at his Raleigh Office at 9 o'clock on May 2, 1985, "all charges against me will be dropped."

I ask him to repeat ""All charges -- Federal, State and local will be dropped," two more times. Agent Pence repeats, "All charges,."

At exactly 9:00 AM, on May 2, I enter FBI Agent Pence's office. Pence, who is standing at his desk flanked by the US flag on one side and the North Carolina flag on the other, motions his head toward two of the plainclothesmen who seize my arms and handcuff me.

"You're under arrest,"

"You said all charges would be dropped if I voluntarily presented myself to you at 9:00 this morning!"

"There were no Federal charges. These men are from the Wake County Sheriff's Office." (If no Federal judges, why is FBI Agent talking/negotiating with me on the phone? If no federal charges by what authority has Pence been threatening me? By what authority did he tell me four times, "All charges would be dropped?" The Government of the United States is corrupt and crooked?

I'm jailed in the Wake County Courthouse, no charges are cited, no Miranda, no phone call, and no option of an attorney is offered. (FBI Agent Pence is the criminal who should have been cuffed and jailed.)

My friend posts my bond – as I recall for $25,000.

Judge "Rusty" Sherrill's Arrest Warrant, dated December 23, 1984, reads;"The undersigned' (Judge Sherrill) "finds that there is probable cause to believe that on or about the date shown, the defendant " unlawfully, willfully, and feloniously did take Shannon Brooke Coleman, a child under the age of 16,, born February 19, 1981, from Cary, North Carolina to Hughesville, PA, with the intent to violate a court order issued by Hon. Russell Sherrill, District Judge, 10th Jud. District of North Carolina. Said court order #CVD 1742, issued on December 17, 1984. Viol. GS 14.3.120 -- Failure to return minor child within 72 hours in violation of a civil court Order."

The record shows the Indictment was not issued until May 28, 1985, meaning Judge Sherrill's Arrest Warrant dated December 23, 1984, was itself "unlawful, willful, and felonious" Judge Sherrill should have been arrested and so charged.

It gets worse much worse. (1) On the date the warrant was issued claiming I had left for Hughesville, PA, I was residing in Wake County. (2) I did not leave from Cary, North Carolina. (3) I did not go to Hughesville, PA, nor have I ever been to Hughesville, PA. (4) I had neither received nor known of any, nor had I been served any such Order issued by Judge Sherrill, therefore I could not have intended to violate an Order which I never saw, and which I suspect was either willfully sent to the wrong address, was fraudulently drafted AFTER the fact, or said Sherrill Order never existed. (5) Rather, I intended to seek asylum from corrupt Jim Crow Wake County judges acting contrary to Shannon's best interests and welfare, (6) There was never a court order stating I had to return my daughter, within 72 hours, or the penalties, if any, for not doing so, (7) If my newly hired attorney and ex-judge had no knowledge of GS 14,320.1. why should I?

The Arrest Warrant was a fraud, based not on an indictment by a grand jury as required by the North Carolina Constitution, but instead, on misinformation personally made by K to her favorite Judge "Rusty."

On advice of a friend, I hire attorney Clarence Kirk, an ex-judge and "good ole boy" from the den of the Democratic Party. He's the same attorney who had won the paternity suit against Wake County DA Riley. He takes my "non-refundable" $10,000 retainer, refuses to assert the "Natural Law" defense suggested to me by Wade Smith, one of the most respected lawyers in North Carolina, and then makes a deal with the Devil -- Wake County District Court Judge Lee – that I undergo a psychological exam, which I'm lead to believe will take a few hours.

But, when I show up for the exam in suit and tie, promising I'll be home for supper, I'm sent upstairs to the jail, processed as an inmate, chained, and sent to a maximum security prison in Salisbury North Carolina, placed in a cell block for murderers, and kept for 52 days, as part of a "secret" 60-90 day sentence, begging the question where in the Bill of Rights, or the North Carolina Constitution, is it written that judges can sentence defendants BEFORE the trial? (Oh, I keep forgetting this is Jim Crow North Carolina, where there is no Rule of Law and no US Constitution, and the North Carolina Constitution is what any judge in the State says it is.)

While in a maximum prison, my attorney fails to return my phone calls, so I ask my oldest daughter to contact him She reports attorney Kirk, didn't tell me the psyche exam was part of a 60-90 day "deal" fearing I wouldn't agree to the exam causing Judge Lee to hit me with a longer sentence

At the trial, a choreographed weeping K recounts her local, national, and international efforts to retrieve

Shannon -- this from the same mother who took her 20 month-old daughter to all night beer bashes and pot parties, who drove home drunk and stoned at 3:15 in the morning, with Shannon in the car – the same mother who, with evil intent, told Shannon, "Your father sexually molested you when you were three years old," and the same mother who lied to Shannon, "Your father almost caused you to have your leg amputated," and who would destroy her daughter's relationship with her father to satiate her own vindictiveness toward him, her daughter's relationship with her father be damned!

K's attorney, pointing to an envelope on the table, asks K, "Are those your receipts for your expenses in finding and bringing back your daughter from Canada?"

"Yes," she sobs."

I whisper to my attorney, "Not unless she bought the plane."

My attorney never questions K, never asks to see the receipts, never lets me testify as to the reasons we sought asylum in Canada, nor allowed me to testify on how happy Shannon had been while away from her mother. My attorney   offers no Natural Law defense as recommended by Wade Smith. In fact he offers no defense, pleads me guilty, and tells the judge I'm sorry for what I did. (In another state. the verdict would have been over-turned by reason of negligent or incompetent representation, but North Carolina is a closed society, beyond the reach of the Constitution of the United States.)

Judge Lee finds me guilty as charged, sentences me to make full restitution of some $7,791.59, orders four years probation, and credit for time served as scripted by conspiratorial Judge, Lee, DA Riley, and attorney .Kirk, withou6t my knowledge or consent.

,K, encouraged by the ease with which she can

manipulate Wake County Judges, in general. Judge "Rusty" Sherrill in particular, Wake County DA Riley, WRAL-TV and the *Raleigh News & Observer,* now goes in for the kill. She sues to have the State of North Carolina terminate my parental rights because I had failed to pay child support while in Canada and while in prison.

This trial, even more contrived, more corrupt and more insidious than the previous travesty, involves Confederate War holdout Judge Bason, John Hall, the attorney Bason hand-picked to represent me, and two young attorneys – one male and one female, who I never knew whether they were representing K or the State of North Carolina.

While I am being questioned on the stand by my attorney, John Hall, and in plain view of Judge Bason, the female attorney repeatedly mouths the words, "You're a liar! You're a liar. You're a liar."

Neither Judge Bason, nor my attorney attempt to stop this blatant harassment, intimidation, and obstruction of justice.

When my attorney asks me. "How much did you make the past 12 months?" I'm shocked. My attorney has suddenly shifted sides and is now prosecuting me!

…I've sold my Stop Smoking clinics, my house, worked briefly for a real estate firm before going to Canada, but was paid nothing, earned no money while in Canada …bought a videographics franchise, since returning, made some money with my associate, but don't know at that moment my share of earnings less the cost of the franchise so I answer truthfully, "I don't know."

Attorney Hall, appointed by presiding judge Bason, on cue, cries, "I ask that the Court grant me permission to withdraw. I can't represent a client who lies on the witness stand."

If the trial smells like a Jim Crow conspiracy, feels like a Jim Crow conspiracy, and sounds like a Jim Crow conspiracy, it's a damn Jim Crow conspiracy – written and directed by Wake County Judge Bason -- the same Judge Bason who appointed Hall to represent me , when I had never requested an attorney.

The ending is as Bason scripted. My parental rights are terminated. The State of North Carolina, which claims title to being a "family values" State, has not only criminalized my paternal instincts to protect my daughter, but now, declares null and void, the simple inalienable biological truth that I am Shannon's father!

Bason compounds his treachery by keeping a bogus Restraining Order in place for so long as I shall live.

K's *News & Observer* and WRAL-TV propaganda blitzkrieg renders me *persona non grata* in Wake County. For example, a woman State psychologist, who I never met, who never witnessed my relationship with Shannon, and who had no knowledge of K's evil acts of alienation of my daughter's affection, publically announces that, "Dr. Coleman is not fit to work with children." (Another adult female fucking me over! Why didn't I sue her for slander? I would have a better chance of suing the US Supreme Court for rigging the 2000 election for Bush II!)

Fleeing down the road to Smithfield, my new Probation Officer, hereafter referred to as "Bitch Barbie," based on her looks and personality, convinced "the Court should have "fried your ass," seeks, by any means -- fair or foul -- to put me back in prison. (Another adult female fucking me over.)

Before she does just that, we "Go west, young man, go west," arriving in Ashville, where I establish residence, a phone number, and report the next day to a

Buncombe County/Asheville Probation Officer, who fills out the transfer papers and gives me seven days to secure employment, which I do -- repossessing used cars for dealers @ $50 dollars per car.

Some weeks later, "Bitch Barbie" swears out a warrant for my arrest for moving to Asheville without her "written permission." (In fact, I'd told Bitch Barbie I was moving to Asheville, to which she made no comment, thus entrapping me to believe she had no objection.)

My Buncombe County probation officer notifies "Bitch Barbie" that I have officially transferred my case to her and that I have complied with all the requirements, including full-time employment

"Bitch Barbie" is unmoved and orders me back to Smithfield (600 miles round trip and lost wages) to stand trial.

The judge rules in my favor, but "Bitch Barbie" tries again several months later, and with the same result. (In any state north of the Mason-Dixon Line other than Utah and Arizona, Bitch Barbie would have been fired for such an outrageous abuse of power.

After repossessing cars for about a year, during which I am attacked by a hammer-wielding house painter and an ex-Clemson University linebacker, I answer a newspaper ad for "tutor" for a 4 year-old boy, who turns out to be autistic.

Initially, the boy has no social speech, can't tell his patents of his needs and wants - he pulls them to the refrigerator -- no pre-school skills, no cognitive ability, and no fine motor skills -- can't hold a pencil or crayon, and his physical skills are limited to hopping from one piece of living room furniture to another like a monkey, or endlessly jumping on his trampoline absent any sign of enjoyment.

After ten months of "tutoring." now five, he can order a hamburger at McDonalds, name common objects and pictures of same, use irregular plurals, answer questions, print his full name, print all 26 letters of the alphabet, print spell and read 50 sight words, draw a face with eyes, nose, mouth, and ears, recognize 9 colors, 5 shapes, numbers from 1 to 1,000, categorize objects and animals according to their characteristics, play catch and throw with a tennis ball from ten feet, hit a pitched ball, and ride a full-size bike, albeit in repetitive circles absent any signs of enjoyment.

In 10 months, he gains 2 years in language, 2 ½ years in gross motor skills, 3 years in fine motor skills, and 2 years in cognitive ability..His IQ was estimated to be in the 60 -70 range.

His father enrolls him in a regular public school first grade.

North Carolina recognizes these precedent-setting increases in ability in a pre-school autistic child by sponsoring me to do state-wide workshops and seminars, right? Wrong! Another psychologist goes behind my back to report to the Licensing Board that I'm practicing psychology without a license.

I rebut by pointing out that the ad was for a "tutor," I was hired as a tutor, worked as a tutor and was paid as a tutor. If there is an ethical breach, it is the Board's demanding that I withhold from the child and his parents any and all skills and training I may have gained as a psychologist.

I hire an attorney. The North Carolina Licensing Board still finds me guilty of practicing psychology without a license. (The State's witness is the boy's father, an urologist trained in India, who had earlier threatened to fire me if I attended my father's funeral, who was angry with me when I told him I was leaving.

and .who refused to pay me when I submitted my 30-days notice.)

Next I secure a job as a school psychologist, (no license required), in Jacksonville, North Carolina, which includes consulting for a class of autistic children.

We, (Wife #3 and her now teenage daughter) rent a cottage at Topsail Beach, about 20 miles from Jacksonville. Wife #3 takes a two-week Florist Class in Atlanta, Georgia, and her 15 year old daughter enrolls as a freshman at the local high school.

The teacher for the class of autistic children, is Susan Maloney, who began flirting the first day I walked into her classroom. She somehow gets my phone number and begins calling me. I'm either jogging on the beach, or not able to get to the phone before wife #3 answers. Susan does not hang up when Wife # 3 answers, nor makes an attempt to hide her identity.

Two months later, I return home from work to find wife #3 and her daughter have gone back to her parents in Williamsport, PA. (This is the third time she has left since the relationship began three months after my separation with K, (wife #2) in 1983.

As Ted Williams would have said, Susan's "pushing real hard," I admit I'm flattered. She's attractive – big seductively treacherous brown eyes, a "fuck me " smile, big boobs, nice firm butt -- attributes which I consciously perceive to justify my reciprocal flirting. It turns out that the real "pull" is of a much more sinister kind. **Susan is more my mother's clone in looks and personality than wife #2 had ever been -- my heretofore 48 year search for my mother has ended!** That's the bad news. There is no good news. Let me explain.

On a Friday evening, December, 1988, I hear a knock on my beach house door. Standing in the open doorway, dressed in jeans, a jacket, and wearing a man's felt hat, with a travel bag over her shoulder, Susan announces, "I'm spending the weekend."

Leaving me speechless and still standing at the open door, she adds, "Cute place you have here," as she goes from room to room as a dog might check out its new surroundings,

"Come here," she calls from the direction of my bedroom, "I have something for you."

She's wearing nothing but a small smile. The sexual assault is from the top position of power and control. The only criterion missing for a charge of rape is I didn't say "no".

Two weeks later, she sends me a card, "Congratulations! We did it! I'm pregnant"

Shock! Numbness..Confusion, then Hallelujah! My fatherhood reborn! 'A second Shannon!' Then, an ice-cold shower – She's married to a Marine Captain, with two kids -- a girl seven or eight, and a boy about two.

I leave Topsail Beach and buy a three bedroom house in Jacksonville. The first night, I awake with cockroaches using my bare chest as their playground.

At 7:38, on the morning of October 16, 1989, she calls from the hospital, "It's a boy!"

Home alone, I'm free to run through the house shouting, "A son! A son! I have a son!"

In such instant delights, lurk its opposite. The Birth Certificate lists the marine as the father and my son as Sean Michael Maloney.

In preparation for the baby's arrival, I had re-carpeted my entire house, retiled the master bath, knocked out an entrance wall, and converted one bedroom into a newly painted nursery furnished with a new crib with hanging toys, changing table, rocking chair, and walls papered with a rainbow motif as the baby's gender was unknown at the time.

I purchase a house around the corner, so Susan and her family can move into mine.

The incontrovertible evidence gleaned from her behavior is that my sole future role is to be "stud service" on demand, while her marine husband is officially credited with my son's paternity.

I'll have none of it. Already I have lost, or had taken from me, three of my children. I will not lose another.

Susan being Catholic, which has no influence on her character or her behavior other than what she does for an hour Sunday mornings, Susan insists on baptizing my son. (Baptizing – that singular act of physical and psychological child abuse perpetrated on helpless vulnerable infants by Christian clerics, under the ruthless ruse of "original sin," when the real purpose is to "mark" the infant as a future cash-paying Christian parishioner.

I draft a Separation Agreement, which. Susan and her husband file on April, 1990. He moves out. I move in – it was my house anyway – the entire transition being as smooth as honey on pancakes.

Too many people discover she lied: I am the father, just as some suspected, and now everyone knows.

Time to run. We both get jobs with Surry County Schools. I buy a chalet on a hillside east of Boone. Her daughter now 10 and son, age four, move with us.

Susan's -- Wife #4's techniques to control me become increasingly erratic and annoying -- demanding sex -- withholding sex, threatening suicide, forsaking the marital bed by bedding downstairs with her daughter. (I replace her with my son convinced I'd got the better of the trade.)

On the morning of March 8, 1994, I hear her sneak into my bedroom, feel her slip Sean, age four, out of bed and listen to her carry him downstairs.

The lingering smell of her treachery permeates my bedroom like cheap perfume.

I get up, dress for work, and descend to the kitchen, where I see Sean dressed as if for church, sitting at the bar eating breakfast cereal with his two half siblings, Kate and Patrick.

Suddenly, Susan attacks me, tears my dress shirt, rams me against the side door, grabs me by my necktie, and drags me to the living room couch, where, still choking me, she jumps on top of me, yelling, "Kate, grab Sean and run to the car!"

I bench press her to the floor, and get to Sean before Kate does.

Susan screams, "He's not yours. He's from a one-night stand at a bar in Wilmington!" as she races across the living room to the phone on my desk… "911? My husband just attacked me – I want him arrested for domestic violence! …Yes, just now… Doc Watson Road – A-frame -- next to last house --Deep Gap!"(Déjà vu – Wife #2)

Holding Sean, I call 911 … "The call you just received from my wife … She's the one who assaulted me. I'm going to file charges. I'm taking my son. We won't be here!"

Having learned the lessons from Wife #2 – K -- not to defend myself lest I be charged with assault, and battery, and that the first one to the lawyer wins, within an hour, my attorney, presented with my torn shirt, secures the judge's signature on an Ex Parte Domestic Violence Protective Order ordering Susan "to immediately leave and stay away from the party's residence."

Just as Borderline Personality K had done, Susan retaliates by getting her lawyer to file a Motion that I'm not Sean's father, forcing me to pay $600.dollars for a paternity test. (My card signed by Susan saying

"Congratulations we did it! I'm pregnant!" is not sufficient to prove Susan's perjury?)

Just as Borderline Personality K had done, Susan has me (twice) investigated by Social Services based on "anonymous tips" that I sexually assaulted Sean. (K filed a Motion I had sexually molested Shannon)

Just as Borderline Personality K had done with Shannon, Susan puts Sean in harm's way: by: (1) Letting Sean and his half-brother play with matches unsupervised, (2) Enabling a "stove fire," while Susan is not home, (3) Enabling Sean to swallow glass while he is left in the care of his 12 year-old half-sister, Kate, (4) Forcing Sean, Kate, and Patrick to "camp out" at night in the yard, so Susan and her boyfriend can fuck inside, (5) Allowing four year-old Sean to watch "R" rated movies, like *Speed,* (6) Allowing Sean and Patrick to roam the streets of Elkin , NC unsupervised, (7) Enabling Sean and Patrick to go swimming unattended -- Sean dives from a diving board into water over his head. (He can't swim.) (8) Susan hits Sean with belts, fly swatters and wooden cooking spoons, leaving bruises on his face visible to me when he returns home from visitations. (Recall, my Borderline mother crammed Ivory Soap into my mouth and whipped me with her ironing cord), and Borderline K took 20 month old Shannon to all-night beer and pot parties and then, while DUI, drove her home, (9) Susan leaving Sean home unsupervised from 5-9, while she works at a Dollar Tree.

Just as Borderline Personality K had done, Susan similarly slanders me to Sean, "Your father is a queer. Other children won't play with you because your father is bad. Your father killed one of his wives. Your Daddy hurt your Mommy and threw her out of the house with no place to go. Your Daddy is sick in the head, Your

Daddy is going to die because he's an old man. The reason your Dad likes you to sleep in his bed, is so he can do funny things to you," and encouraging each of her new boyfriends to repeat the same slanderous statements to Sean

Just as Borderline Personality K had done, Susan turns every visitation exchange into a traumatic event for Sean, trying to provoke a fight by cussing me, calling me a "faggot" and worse, encouraging each new live-in boyfriend to start a fight, refusing to present Sean for court-ordered visitations and involving the police in visitations.

Like K, Susan submits three pages of items she claims were hers "before the marriage," when, in fact, she moved in with only a few clothes.

Both K and Susan are dedicated to the proposition, "The best lie wins,." and both were psychopathic liars, as was my mother

August 2, 1995, Surry County (NC) DSS finds Susan guilty of neglect – "abusing the minor child during visitation." (Why had Wake County DSS failed to punish K for her abuse of Shannon? Because there are two North Carolina's – one east – bad, and one west– good?)

September1996, Watauga County District Court Judge Leavell awards me sole legal and physical custody of Sean, orders Susan to pay me child support in the amount of $337.48, of which $90 is credited for medical and dental insurance, (which Susan immediately cancels) and orders Susan to reimburse me for any uninsured medical or dental bills. (She never does.)

Under identical circumstances 14 years earlier, (1) Wake County Judges allow into evidence K's statement that I sexually molested Shannon, but the Watauga County Judge reads Susan's two claims I sexually molested Sean as alienation of affection and orders Susan to undergo therapy and supervised visitation (2) Wake County judges and magistrates prosecuted me for incidents of assault either committed, or instigated, by K, yet, for an identical incident of assault instigated by Susan, a Watauga County judge issues an Ex Parte Domestic Violence Petition ordering Susan to vacate the marital residence and restraining her from contacting Sean and me. (3) Fourteen years ago, acting in K's interests and against the best interests of the child – Shannon -- Wake County judges force me to protect Shannon from them and her mother by seeking asylum in Canada, yet a Watauga County Judge, acting in Sean's best interests, awards me sole physical and legal custody and orders Susan to pay me child support.

Yes there are indeed two North Carolina's.-- East – bad, West – good.

Sean comes home from school his first day at Waccamaw Academy crying because his male classmates banished him to go play with the girls because he didn't know how to play soccer.

With father/son after school and weekend "kick-arounds," Sean is soon the best player in his group and is asked to play on a club team of 6-7 year-olds.

His first game is to be on a Saturday when Susan is due to have visitation.

I offer to pay for her motel for Friday night so she can watch Sean play his first game that Saturday morning, and then take him for her weekend visitation,

She pauses then answers, "If Sean thinks more of soccer than he does his mother, I don't care if I never see him again!" Slam!

She never does.

A year later, guardian ad litem Kay Dickey writes to the Judge that "Sean's mother is intent on severing all ties with her son Sean." (She is abandoning

Sean at age four as my mother abandoned me when I was four. Scary!

In 1996, I warn my attorney that Susan will refuse to comply with the Court's Order. By the time Sean turns 18, Susan owes me arrearages of $20,000. – a "dead-beat mom," *n'est pas*?

Courts allow three-year reviews of child support, but Susan has gone through two more husbands, used nine different names and 11 different addresses, thereby escaping all three-year reviews. (I hire a private detective who finds her living in Lexington, Virginia as Susan Hogan.

Meanwhile, I attempt to get Social Services in Florida, and New Hampshire, where Sean and I lived, North Carolina, where the original Order was issued, and Nevada and Virginia, where Susan lived at the time of the filing, to enforce Judge Leavell's child support Order.

Florida declines, claiming no jurisdiction despite the fact Sean and I lived in Florida 2001-2004.. New Hampshire (Alabama of the northeast) tells me I would have to file in Virginia, where Susan resides, even though Susan waived her right to immunity from prosecution in New Hampshire by answering my New Hampshire Complaint, and, despite the fact that my 14th Amendment right to equal protections under the laws would be violated by forcing me to file, travel, and prosecute my case in Virginia, where I would be subject to the same Jim Crow lawlessness and corrupt judges encountered in Wake County, North Carolina.

Indeed, the Rockbridge Virginia Circuit Court, the Clerk of Court, the female judge, the female attorney representing Susan, and the Virginia Court of Appeals, acting as a criminal enterprise under R.I.C.O., conspired as follows: (1) At the Hearing on June 12, 2008, the woman judge denied me a Hearing on any of my

Motions and Petitions to Modify and collect arrearages.
(2) Instead, the woman judge denied me my due process
right to participate in the Hearing on Virginia DCSE's
Motion to Amend, which Susan's woman attorney
turned into a verbal Motion to demand my tax records.
(3) The woman judge issued a Summons for me to
appear back in Lexington, Virginia on September 11,
2008, as the now *de facto* Defendant instead of Plaintiff.
(4) Susan's woman attorney, in league with the woman
judge, fraudulently claim that the Summons is an Order
for my tax records, bank statements, and record of
"monies spent on minor child in 2008," when Susan's
attorney and the judge both knew no such order was
included in, or attached to, the Summons. (5) On August
19, 2008, Susan's female attorney files a fraudulent
Motion to Dismiss -- actually Virginia DCSE's case,
not Susan Hogan's -- claiming I had failed to produce
tax returns by August 11, 2008, when Susan's attorney
knew no such Order existed and that I had provided tax
records to said attorney and the Clerk of Court on
August 31, 10 days in advance of the September 11,
Hearing. (6) At the telephonic Hearing, on September
11th Hearing, as allowed by the Special Evidentiary
Provisions of the Uniform Family Support Act, the same
woman judge violates my 5th and 14th Amendment rights
to due process and my 14th Amendment right to equal
protections under the laws by refusing me a Hearing on
my motions to Modify and for Arrearages. (7) The
woman judge dismisses my case against Susan for
$20,000.00 arrearages, which was, in fact, Virginia's
DCSE's case, claiming I failed to comply with an Order
for tax records which were: (a) Irrelevant to either case,
and (b) To comply with an order which never existed.
(8) The woman judge compounds her egregious
misconduct and multiple criminal acts of obstruction of
justice, by ordering me to pay "punitive damages" of

$1,000, with $500 going to the judge's "sorority sister" and partner in crime – Susan's attorney, and $500 to the Virginia DCSE attorney. (9) The woman judge wrongly instructs me I have 10 days to appeal. (10) The woman judge committed felony Obstruction of Justice by withholding mailing the notice of the 10 days to Appeal until the 10 days had lapsed, to wit, I received the Judge's Order dated the day of the Hearing, September 11, 2008, but not post-marked until September 23. 2008, two days after the 10 days elapsed, and received by me on September 25, 2008, or seven days after the 10 days elapsed. (It should be noted that this woman Rockbridge Circuit Court Judge, to avoid detection, scratched her signature on all her orders so as to make her name illegible and, absent the typed name underneath as practiced by judges not needing to hide their "high crimes and misdemeanors." (11) Deputy Rockbridge Circuit Court Clerk Tracy Smith wrote "…too much time has passed and you are unable to appeal that decision," (12) I wrote to the court on October 10, 15, 22, 27, 31, and November 6, protesting the denial of my 5th and 14th Amendment due process right to appeal and my Constitutional right to be given equal protections under the laws. Each time, my Notice to Appeal is returned to me, (13) By Order dated November 25, 2008, the same woman Rockbridge County Circuit Court Judge rules my Notice of Appeal is "summarily" dismissed. Again her name on the Order is deliberately illegible, but not able to hide the fact of her commission of judicial over-reach, and acting without jurisdiction to do so, thereby inviting charges of impeachment, and treason and conspiring to participate in a criminal enterprise as defined by R.I.C.O – the Racketeer Influenced and Corrupt Organizations Act

All the Virginia parties were tried, convicted, and currently serving time in federal prison along with the Wake County judges, right?

Wrong! This is the South. Jim Crow still nests in the Wake County NC and Rockbridge County, VA courthouses – (A name for a book I must write, along with another book already started titled, "Dirty Judges," which I can't finish, because so many new dirty judges keep popping up that what started to be about the exceptional corrupt judge is now about the typical judge,)

Naïve ignorant me! Why would I expect to find, judicial fairness, political impartiality, honesty, and integrity at the state and local levels when the majority of the judges on the US Supreme Court were appointed by Conservative Republican Presidents for the sole unlawful purpose of installing their radical neo-Conservative- theocracy on the American body politic?

In September 1996, I begin as a psychology professor at Southeastern Community College, in Whiteville, North Carolina where, while going to, or coming from, a baseball field where Sean is playing, I pass Karen, one of K's weird, spacey underlings from long ago. She too, is on her way to, or from the baseball field with her son, about the same age as Sean.

I don't recognize her the first time, but my taut gut and rapid shallow breathing signals "trouble."

Some days later I see her again at the same ball field   with her son. It is Karen, who I remember as a flighty follower of fads, for whom K once "volunteered" that I would pay for a week's vacation at Emerald Isle for Karen and her family during which I would counsel Karen's husband, purportedly dying of cancer. (Karen's home yin and yang diet remedies having failed).

Karen's affect always seems disconnected – exaggerated -- too sweet, too soft spoken as if a mask for a darker, (yang) malevolent, evil side … I wonder if I'm being used by K and Karen as a cover for Karen's failed attempts to save her husband, who didn't seem to be aware of his imminent death, or am I am an unwilling and unwitting co-conspirator in the death of Karen's husband?

He subsequently died. He was only in his early 30's. (I much later as told that Karen's daughter also died under unclear circumstances.

Karen marries two or three more times, this last time to a hospital administrator in Whiteville, North Carolina.

Meanwhile, the *Fayetteville Observer's* headline accuses my College President of misappropriating $364.000, which the NC legislators had earmarked for faculty salaries, but which my College President allegedly appropriated for projects of his own.

Volunteering no explanation at a faculty meeting, I ask the President as to the disbursement of the $364,000. He answers by inviting me to his office, where, in the presence of one of his sycophants, he fires me and tells me someone else will be teaching my classes to finish the semester. . (This is the south where for 400 years the function of its institutions is to exploit and control its African-American males. In 1998 North Carolina, no one, but NO ONE questions "the man," especially not an outsider like me.

I sue the College and the President for wrongful termination.

Karen, acting upon K's instructions and instigation, informs the College President of my felony conviction in 1985. The State's attorney settles with me for pennies on the dollar arguing that the College would have fired me anyway as soon as the College learned of the felony.

From Shannon 13 years later, l learn that K not only took full credit for getting me fired, but bragged to Shannon for having done so. According to Shannon, K told Shannon, "Your father had been stalking the children of Karen McDonald, (If so, why was I never charged?), "because she testified against him in the custody hearing." (Karen did not testify at that or any other \ Hearing), and that "Karen got him (me) kicked out of town," (I was never kicked out of town. In fact, I stayed around long enough to investigate and write a book about one of my students charged with the death of her 17 month-0lod son, titled, *Justice for Baby Josh* -- Amazon).

K also told Shannon I was kicked out of town "because I had already scared the Dean's daughter" (To my knowledge, the Dean either didn't have a daughter, or said daughter did not live in Whiteville), "by leaving short stories about seducing and then murdering a woman fitting her description on his computer." (How could the absent Dean's daughter read anything on my computer? On what basis would the Dean's daughter have gained access to my computer? I never wrote short stories.)

Karen, according to K, said that " the boys all went to play basketball except Sean, who sat with "creepy loyalty" at his father's knee, while the other boys went out to play"(The sport was baseball, and Sean was one the top players even though he was one of the youngest, and played regularly in every game and practice.)

The only thing "creepy' is the extent of K's mental disorder, the evidence of which being that she would tell such outrageous and outlandish lies, and do so to Shannon.

(There may not be a rule of law or a US Constitution in North Carolina, but the Peter Principle rules absolutely – The felonious College President gets promoted to the State's Community College Headquarters in Raleigh.)

Thirty years after the State of North Carolina criminalized my paternal instincts to protect Shannon, costing me at least $2, 250,000.00, in lost income, and incalculable emotional and psychological injury, while sitting at my computer, I receive the following e-mail:

"Hi there, I looked around your site for clues or dates, but I assume that you no longer operate via http://authorsbooks direct. However, I'm definitely interested in your publications. If this is an active e-mail account, won't you please respond? Thank you for your time and attention. Scarlette Shannon."

I blink – shake my head. I read the e-mail again-- – a third time.

'After 30 years of missing my little girl, can this be my Shannon? I last saw her sitting on some stone wall outside a building – probably a courthouse – in March, 1985!'

I read her message three more times. 'Who else could it be? But Shannon was her first name. I picked it as a tribute to her mother's parents and because the name sounded soft and sonorous.'

Over the next several months Shannon reveals that **she hasn't contacted me for 30 years because of the things K told her about me,** for example, K told Shannon, "Your father tried to kill his first wife and their two girls. Your father sexually molested you when you were three. Your father caused you to almost have your leg amputated. Your father never wanted you. I had to trick him into getting pregnant. Your father was sodomized by his mentor in seminary school. Your father was always preoccupied with little boys" – all such outrageous lies could only be uttered by an evil tongue!

Shannon says she loves me and apologizes for ever believing her "lying and just plain evil mother."

I find no solace in recalling that 30 years ago, I warned Wake County judges that K will physically and mentally destroy Shannon as the unwanted progeny of my scorned sperm. I find no solace in recalling that 30 years ago, I warned Wake County judges and lawyers that K's plot to make Shannon hate and fear her father was to avenge both Shannon and I for having compromised – threatened K's Borderline Personality Disorder control.

Shannon's e-mails next report, "Honestly, I feel poisoned. Mom had me pumped full of Thorazine by the 7th grade and locked me up in psychiatric hospitals in middle and high school for months at a time, until the insurance ran out. Because I seemed sad and rebellious, she locked me up – usually the only kid without a police record or bad grades. Name an anti-psychotic drug, or an SSRI, or anything trendy, and I've been convinced to swallow it . then pretend to take it for a few more times – I simply do not like taking pills, or seeing doctors, and I don't think I'm sick or damaged. I was raised under the guidance of dozens of other psychiatrists – doctors who sat through hours of my mom's theatrics without protest."

Jim Crow Wake County judges Bullock, Sherrill, Carswell, Lee and Bason and lawyers Parker, Hall, and Kirk, DA Riley and the two Attorneys from the Attorney General's office prosecuting the termination of my parental rights case, must all be held accountable for **aiding and abetting K's 30 years of the psychological and emotional trauma done to Shannon by her mother -- 30 years of making Shannon an institutionalized mental health patient, and 30 years of poisoning Shannon's relationship with her father** – collateral damage in order to punish a "white nigger" from the land of the hated Kennedy's, collateral damage to save the political neck of Wake County DA Riley, and the Wake County Democratic Party – collatoral damage just so Judge "Rusty" Sherrill could gain sexual favors from K? (Geez, I only had sex with K six times in six years and even then, not one was memorable – certainly not worth a judgeship.) All of the above?

After many months of pondering how I can again – with better results – help Shannon free herself from her ruinous and "evil" mother, I sue K for Slander, alleging that Kay stated as facts to an unprivileged third party, (Shannon) "Your father sexually molested you when your were three years old. Your father tried to kill his ex-wife and their two daughters. Your father was awarded sole custody of his son only because he and the boy's mother beat each other so badly that both were hospitalized, but because your father was released before the mother, he was awarded custody. Your father would only have sex through a hole in the sheet after disrobing under the covers, so I deceived" your father about birth-control pills to conceive you. I wanted a child. Your father never wanted you. He was disappointed that he had a daughter because he always seemed inappropriately preoccupied with little boys. Your father, during his "orphanhood (sic) had been sodomized by his mentor in seminary school. You almost had to have your leg amputated" because blunt-force trauma caused the streptococcus bacteria to pool in your ankle after a fall at Pullen Park in Raleigh, because your father had taken you to Tweetsie Park in Boone, NC, instead of the Emergency Room in Raleigh."

Under North Carolina law, a statement is defamatory (slanderous) " if it is so egregious as to presume harm to the plaintiff without the need to prove that harm.

K, who still seems to have a friend or friends in high places in the Wake County courts – (I suspect ex-long time Wake County District Court Judge "Rusty," Sherrill) , answers my Complaint by filing **21** redundant, "bad faith," and trivial Motions between June 2 and July 28, 2014, including **SIX** First Requests for Production of Documents, all dated June 2, 2014, two identical Motions to Compel on two different dates, her Motion to Dismiss, her first Motion for Summary Judgment and her Motion for Protection Order alleging that my responsive pleadings to K's motions caused K "to be placed in fear of continued harassment that rises to such a level as to inflict substantial emotional distress." (New Wake County Courthouse, but same old corrupt criminal Jim Crow Wake County judges.)

K's Motion for Summary Judgment, is not only grossly defective on its face, to wit, it fails to show that there are no issues of material fact in dispute, as required by NCRCP Rule 56, but adds six additional issues, all of which are disputed in my Complaint and must therefore be stricken.

Female Wake County Superior Court Judge Elaine Bushfan must, therefore, on her own initiative – *sua sponte* – MUST dismiss Kay's Motion for Summary Judgment as defective, improper, and being at odds with the requirements of NCRCP Rule 56.

But this is Wake County North Carolina. Female Judge Bushfan violates my 5th and 14th Amendment due process and equal protection under the laws, by forbidding me to question or challenge K's testimony, allows K to present unchallenged slanderous, inflammatory prejudicial, irrelevant, hearsay and perjured testimony, for example, " The Plaintiff (me) abducted our daughter on December 24, 1984, when she was 3 years old because he didn't want to pay child support."

Perjury, perjury, and more perjury. I was never charged or convicted of abducting Shannon. We fled North Carolina to protect Shannon from her evil mother and corrupt Jim Crow Wake County judges, who put her in harm's way, and child support was current.

K next testifies, "Any statements I made about the Plaintiff (me) to family or friends was limited to matters of public record of the kidnapping"

K knew, and Judge Bushfan should have known, I was never charged with "kidnapping," therefore, there could be no public record of kidnapping my daughter, meaning K's every repetition of the word "kidnapping," constituted another act of fraud, defamation, slander, and perjury..

Judge Bushfan as an officer of the Court was duty-bound to charge and arrest K for perjury.

It gets worse – much worse. Judge Bushfan allows K to present hearsay evidence in the form of a sworn Affidavit of adult daughter Shannon, now 33 years old, with the Certificate of Service signed by K, which should have caused Judge Bushfan to ask, How did Shannon's Affidavit come to be in K's possession? Was K present while Shannon wrote her Affidavit? On what basis did Shannon surrender her Affidavit to K? How did Shannon know to use the same format and court captions which K used in her pleadings, and how did Shannon know the case number?

The incontrovertible answer is that **K is guilty of: (a)Felonious witness tampering, (U.S.C. 18 #1512 "Whoever knowingly uses intimidation, threatens, or corruptly persuades another person with the intent to influence any person in an official proceeding shall be fined under this title or imprisoned not more than 20 years or both. (b) Felonious "intimidating or**

interfering with witness" (NC Statute #14-226 – Class G felony). (c) Filing fraudulent reports to court officials, and judges, NC Statute #14-225 – Class 2 misdemeanor. (d) Perjury. (NC General Statute 14-209, "If any person shall willfully and corruptly commit perjury in any courts of the State shall be punished as a Class F felon). (e) Felonious subornation of perjury, (N C Statutes #14-209 and #14-210, "any person, by any means, procures another person to commit such willful and corrupt perjury, in sworn affidavits, that person shall be punished as a Class I felon."

Judge Bushfan, as an officer of the court, is duty-bound to charge and arrest K for the violations of State law as described above, and MUST dismiss her Motion for Summary Judgment, as being fatally flawed according to NCRCP Rule 56.

But this is Wake County North Carolina. Female Judge. Bushfan not only grants K's fraudulent, perjured, slanderous and defective Motion for Summary Judgment, thereby dismissing my Complaint of Slander, Defamation, and Alienation in its entirety, but next conspires with the Clerk of Wake County Superior Court and the Clerk of the North Carolina Court of Appeals to "disappear" my Notice of Appeal, thereby immunizing Bushfan against being Reversed on Appeal!

Emboldened by her ability to manipulate and control Wake County Judges and Court officials, K next persuades female Judge Jennifer Green to grant K's Petition for a Domestic Violence Protective Order, when Judge Green knew, or should have known, **there has been no domesticity in 30 years** – I have had no contact with K since 1984, and therefore no "violence" – domestic or otherwise, for which the Petitioner needs protection.

Two weeks later, at the Hearing (K is now represented by a female Public Defender.

Wait a cotton-pickin' minute! Records show K's household income to be $117,000, and her house valued at $276, 524, with equity at $105,000, begging the question, how did K qualify for a Public Defender? By filing another false report? Friends (ex- judge "Rusty Sherrill) interfering? Female judges and female court officials engaging in gender meddling to favor K? All of the above?)

K's justification for her Complaint of Domestic Violence against me includes K's perjured and slanderous statement that I "kidnapped' Shannon in 1984, which K knew to be perjured and slanderous, and proffered to Judge Green for the sole propaganda and inflammatory purpose of inciting the judge to sign the Domestic Violence Protection Order, in turn, to prevent me from having any contact with Shannon, my only witness..

I file a new Complaint (case # 14-CV-013161) against K for the defamation and slander she committed in her current pleadings, affidavits, motions, and testimony in the Complaint Judge Bushfan just dismissed in its entirety.

The US Supreme Court had long ago concluded, "It had long been clearly established law that the Fourth Amendment prohibits a police officer' (or Petitioner K) "from manufacturing probable cause by knowingly including false statements in a warrant affidavit."

Female Judge Green knew, or should have known, no such connection exits between events alleged 30 years ago and K's current Petition for Domestic Violence Protection Order. Therefore, Judge Green must deny K's Petition as a matter of law.

Instead, "Jane Crow" Judge Green checks the box "The Defendant"(me) "made threats to seriously injure or kill," (K).

When? Where? How? In what criminal court was I tried? What were the terms of my sentence?

Judge Green never asks? Why not? On what basis did Green base her charge? Gender discrimination? K's judge "Rusty's orders? Both?

Judge Green next checks the box: "(x) "inflicted serious injuries upon the plaintiff," and in Judge Green's handwriting she wrote, "strangled."

Now Judge Green must explain how I "strangled" K, when "strangled" means to kill by strangulation." But K is alive -- so alive she files the false report to Judge Green that she was killed by strangulation.

.In what court was I convicted for having strangled K? When? How long was I sentenced? Judge Green got answers BEFORE she wrote the word "strangled.' right? No? Then Judge Green committed criminal fraud and must be disbarred, impeached, and ordered to pay me damages for injuries I sustained due to Judge Green's criminal acts. Maybe outside the South, but not in criminally corrupt Wake County courts.

Next, the Domestic Violence Consent Order is granted by a third female judge – "Jane Crow" Judge M.P..Eagles, who charges: (1) "For the past two years, the defendant (me) placed in fear of continued harassment that rises to such a level as to inflict substantial emotional distress." (K's documented **21 motions** filed against me from June 2, to July 28 – 56 days, or a motion every other business day, are examples of K's fear of my harassment? K's **21 motions and redundant and identical pleadings don't constitute "harassment" of me?** (2) Female Judge Eagles writes

Kay is "terrified" of me because there is no basis for my lawsuits and their sole purpose is to harass and torment" (K.)

I concede K may indeed be "terrified" – terrified that if my case ever goes to trial, the good citizens of Wake County North Carolina will hold K accountable for the two lives she has destroyed by her **30 years of lies, perjured testimony, malicious slander, perverse and destructive alienation of her child's affection for her father, and for having manipulated police, judges, the *News and Observer* and WRAL-TV in service of her evil and wicked plot to crucify me.`**

Oh, I forgot. "Jane Crow" Judge Eagles is just another corrupt Wake County North Carolina judge, (recently elected to the Court of Appeals).

Next, third female Judge Eagles, absent probable cause, orders: "The Defendant (me) shall stay away from the plaintiff's residence, and place of work, and shall be arrested if Defendant violates this provision," thereby violating my Fourth Amendment protection against warrants without probable cause. "The defendant is prohibited from possessing or receiving or purchasing a firearm," violating my Second Amendment right to bear arms, and my right to defend myself against K, who is emotionally unstable, carries the diagnosis of Borderline Personality Disorder, which can include murder of her children or husband.

"Jane Crow" Judge Eagles , guided by the "Peter Principle' rather than the Rule of Law, since moved up to the NC Court of Appeals, knew K had just committed multiple acts of perjury for which Judge ,Eagles, as an officer of the courts, should have **arrested K pursuant to NC General Statute 14-209, as a Class F felony, (North Carolina General Statute #14-209; If any person shall willfully and corruptly commit**

perjury...in any courts of the State ...every person so offending shall be punished as a Class F felon,")

By failing to act as a sworn officer of the Court, Judge Eagles invites charges of corruption, judicial interference, judicial partiality, gender discrimination, felonious subornation of perjury, and acting "under the color of law," to violate my 14th Amendment right to "equal protection under the laws.

On that same afternoon following Judge Eagles' morning signing of the Domestic Violence Protection Order, "terrified" K files a Motion to Dismiss, a second Motion for Summary Judgment and a Motion for Relief from Frivolous Filings, in a **three pound package of over 300 pages of irrelevant, frivolous, fraudulent, and pejorative pleadings, motions and exhibits, leading a reasonable and prudent person to conclude K had been told in advance by a Court "insider" that the judge would be granting K's fraudulent Protection Order stipulating I would be barred from all contact with K -- prohibited from responding to her motions and denied my Fifth Amendment due process right to defend myself!**

Meanwhile, entrapped by the criminally conspiratorial acts of "Jane Crow" -- Wake County female Judges Bushfan, Green, and Eagles, female Trial Court Coordinators, and the female Clerk of Court, I file a Motion to Continue asking the Court to consider that I am being given 10 days to respond to three pounds – over 300 pages of three motions and 28 multiple page Exhibits which, even if I do respond *pro se*, I will be held in Contempt of Court.

By Order dated November 7, the Senior Resident Superior Court Judge Donald Stephens injects himself into the case by denying my request to extend time. No reason or explanation is provided. (Three months earlier, on July 18, 2014, K requests, and is granted, on the spot by Assistant Clerk of Court O'Neal, (not Senior Resident Superior Court Judge Stephens), her motion to Continue, in which she claims, "I have to go out of town for approximately 2 weeks to care for a relative who is ill." (K's only relative is our 33 year-old daughter Shannon, who upon information and belief, resides in Wilmington, NC, and who was not so ill she couldn't get to Durham the day before (July 17) to draft and sign her Affidavit against me and in support of K.)

If it looks like a corrupt criminal conspiracy, feels like a corrupt criminal conspiracy, and smells like a corrupt criminal conspiracy by these "Jim and Jane Crow" Wake County judges, the Clerk of Court, Court staff, and the Court of Appeals to favor K and defeat my Complaint against her, it must be a corrupt criminal conspiracy, and it must be being managed, and orchestrated by a long time court insider.

I put my money on Ex-Wake County District Court Judge Russell "Rusty" Sherrill, who is known to have taken an improper" personal interest in K's cases before him, had acted "extra-judiciously" in her favor in a case, was allegedly seen with K at a Raleigh night club, and who was, and perhaps still is, allegedly in a sexual relationship with K, or at least directing a cover-up of that relationship./

In preparation for the 330 mile-round trip to Raleigh for the Hearing on Monday, November 17, I take the vehicle I would be driving to a mechanic on November13.

The next morning, the mechanic calls to notify me that my motor has a "blown head gasket," possibly causing a "warped head," and in either case, the vehicle "is not drivable."

That same day, I call the Clerk of Court's Office, who informs me the Court has no Fax, so I mail a copy of my Motion to Continue and a copy of the mechanic's bill, via Priority Mail for Monday delivery, stating my car "is not drivable"

That Monday morning, I again call the Clerk of Court. This time I'm given the Fax number I'd been told didn't exist. I Fax my Motion to Continue, a copy of the mechanic's statement and Notice that I mailed the same information that Friday via "Priority "Urgent" Mail" for Monday delivery. (There is not train and the only bus would arrive too late and leave too early.).

By Order dated November 19th, Judge Gregory McGuire writes "…Plaintiff (me) did not file a written response to Defendant's motions." (Judge McGuire knew, or should have known from the file, Judges Green and Eagles had signed a Protection Orders dated October 23, prohibiting me from "having any contact, written or otherwise, with K, including those involving legal matters not drafted and signed by a licensed NC Attorney")

Judge McGuire compounds his "extraordinary" unconstitutional and criminal judicial mischief, by conducting a Hearing without the Plaintiff (me) being present, thereby denying me 5th Amendment right to due process, my 14th Amendment right to equal protection of the laws and Sections 18 and 19 of the NC Constitution.

McGuire should have re-calendared the Hearing as being "best judicial practices," or dismissal "without prejudice" as his choice of last resort,

For his gross and felonious obstruction of justice,, Judge McGuire should have been arrested, jailed, and impeached.

But, not "We ARE the law" judges in Wake County, North Carolina. "The law is what we say it is!"{

K's new Motion for Summary Judgment alleges that Exhibits from 30 years ago establish that there is no genuine issue of material fact" in dispute," in the current case.

Bull shit! Judge McGuire knew, as did K, that a litigant cannot argue that exhibits of 30 years ago prove the current case is without disputed genuine issues of material facts, meaning McGuire, just as Judge Bushfan before him, must dismiss K's Motion for Summary Judgment as a matter of law! (Maybe in another court in another part of North Carolina, but not in Jim Crow Wake County, where all the laws are "local.")

Included in K's exhibits is a copy of the State psychologist's Report of my evaluation done in 1985, as ordered by Judge Lee and marked "Confidential" which begs the question, how did the "Confidential" State's report get in K's hands? More Judge Sherrill's meddling – acting outside his jurisdiction? In any event, the Report is ,irrelevant, immaterial, imfmammatory, and prejudicial, which McGuire must declare inadmissible as a matter of law. He didn't of course, making him inlwful -- a criminal.

K next asserts "…**the statements by the Defendant' (K) of which the Plaintiff (me) complains in this action are true, and were made in the course of the proceedings and filings before this Court and thus are privileged."**

Not so fast! **North Carolina law offers no "privileged" court testimony, meaning K just hung herself -- K just admitted to having made the slanderous defamatory statements just as I alleged in my original Complaint, which Judge Bushfan dismissed!**

Judge McGuire, as an officer of the court, ,is duty-bound to charge and prosecute K for having committed multiple acts of felonious fraud, perjury, suborning perjury, and obstruction of justice, must reinstate my original Complaint, grant my second Complaint for slander, and award me the damages I requested, as a matter of law.

I keep forgetting this is Jim Crow Wake County North Carolina, KKK eastern North Carolina – Jesse Helms country, where instead of following the Rule of Law, Judge McGuire rules: "The Defendant's (K's) Motion for Summary Judgment is GRANTED and this matter" (My Complaint against Kay for Slander and Defamation) is dismissed with prejudice."

Wow! Is this the kind of treacherous injustice and tyranny North Carolina's African-Americans have had to deal with on a daily basis for 400 years? And we criticize injustices in Russia, China, and North Korea? These judges insist we call them "Honorable!" They must mean as in "honor among thieves."

It gets worse. Much worse. At the Hearing on K's Motion for Summary Judgment, Judge McGuire also hears K's Motion for Relief from Frivolous Filings.

Again, for the reasons already cited, I could not be present at this Hearing, which should have been re-calendared, or dismissed without prejudice.

Not according to Judge McGuire's Rules. To give K an unfair and gratuitous advantage, McGuire, under the color of law," holds the Hearing based solely on K's pleadings, exhibits, and testimony, in an egregious violation of my First, Fifth, Seventh, and Fourteenth Amendment Constitutional rights and protections, and my Section 18 and 19 rights under the North Carolina Constitution.

K's stated purpose for her Motion is "To put an end to the deluge of frivolous, vexatious, and fraudulent filings made in 2013 and 2014 by the Plaintiff" (me)

The record will show that **K filed 21 frivolous, vexatious, and fraudulent filings between June 2 and July, 28, 2014.** Furthermore, the majority of my filings were legitimate answers, and responses to K's "deluge" of filings – one every other business day during a 56-day period in the summer of 2014.

Judge McGuire justifies his Draconian incursion into pre-Magna Charta English law by decreeing "Plaintiff (me) has filed numerous frivolous and unwarranted documents with several courts over the last 18 months." (According to whom? McGuire? K? Where is it written that a single presiding judge in any of these prior cases dismissed a single case as being "frivolous and unwarranted"? There is not one. (I argue that the number of cases, rather than being "vexatious" show how corrupt the courts of the United States have become.)

Undeterred by facts or the law, Judge McGuire enters the following Findings of Fact and Conclusions of Law: "The lawsuits filed by Defendant (K) against Plaintiff (me) both in this and other courts, have either been dismissed or are frivolous and without merit."

Apparently, Judge McGuire fraudulently signed his name to an Order he neither wrote not proofed, because (1) **Kay is the Defendant being sued, not the Plaintiff filing the lawsuit**, (2) A case dismissed does not prove frivolity. To the contrary as can be seen in my Wake County court cases "dismissed" may describe judicial corruption, conspiracy to commit fraud and corruption and criminal behavior on the part of judges, (3) Neither K nor Judge McGuire cite a single case in which the judge in one of my cases dismissed for "frivolity," or being without merit. (4) Multiple case filings may represent the extent of the injustice in the states in which the cases were filed. (5) Having failed to identify a single case which a judge ruled frivolous or without merit, K's Motion and McGuire's Order are themselves frivolous and fraudulent.

McGuire's cup of arrogance, hubris, and illegal judicial partiality running over, McGuire plunges forward declaring, "Plaintiff (me) "has represented to this and other courts in which he has made filings that he is indigent, and it is unlikely that plaintiff (me) has sufficient resources to pay costs or other monetary sanctions that may be imposed on him." (And, why Judge McGuire, would monetary sanctions be imposed on me when the evidence shows not one of my filings has been heretofore deemed frivolous or without merit?

Furthermore, as any judge except McGuire knows, noting past acts is considered, prejudicial and therefore omitted by the rules of evidence.

McGuire continues his criminal obstruction of justice and his assault on the Constitutions of the United States and North Carolina, by ruling, "Accordingly, the imposition of monetary sanctions against Plaintiff (me) will not dissuade him from his conduct."

And what conduct is that Judge McGuire? Your conduct aiding and abetting Defendant K, who just admitted to having made the outrageous slanderous and defamatory statements as alleged in my Complaint, to wit, that I 'kidnapped' my daughter," that I "sexually molested my daughter when she was 3? That I "tried to kill and did "strangle" the defendant? That "conduct, Jim Crow Judge McGuire?"

Judge McGuire, in his rush to do a favor for an "interested party"– presumably K's "bedfellow" -- ex-Wake County District Court Judge "Rusty" Sherrill, neglects, or ignores, the last paragraph of K's Motion for Summary Judgment, in which K admits "the (slanderous and defamatory) "statements made" by K of which the Plaintiff (me) complains in this action "are true, and were made in the course of proceedings and filings before this Court and thus are privileged."

Now Judge McGuire please explain to the good citizens of Wake County how my suing K for the slanderous statements she admits to uttering represents a "frivolous and unwarranted filing"…We're all waiting, Judge McGuire …Oh, you think the Scalia's – now

Robert's Conservative US Supreme Court has your back? You got me there.

Setting aside the North Carolina Rules of Civil Procedure, North Carolina statutes and laws, and the Constitutions of North Carolina and the United States, Judge McGuire swore to uphold, he continues his criminal and fraudulent assault on my rights and protections by ruling, (1) "Plaintiff (me) shall obtain the prior written approval of the Senior Resident Superior Court Judge of the county in which the action would be filed prior to filing any *pro se* action of any type in the General Court of Justice that concerns or relates to the Defendant (K), and any allegation raised by Plaintiff in the complaint filed in this action." (2). "In seeking permission to file, Plaintiff (me) shall submit to the Senior Resident Superior Court Judge of the County where the action would be filed, a copy of this Order, a complete copy of any proposed filing, and a verification that the statements in the proposed filing are true, except those matters stated as being made upon information and belief." (3) The Clerk of Superior Court is hereby directed not to accept papers submitted by Plaintiff in violation of the Court's Gatekeeping Order." (4) "A violation of this Order by Plaintiff, or by any person acting on behalf of, or in consort with, the Plaintiff shall be considered contempt and may be sanctioned accordingly, except that this Order shall not apply to any filing submitted on behalf of the Plaintiff by an attorney licensed to practice law in the State of North Carolina." (5) "A copy of this Order shall be delivered to the Wake County Clerk of Court."

Has a more outrageous criminal assault on a US citizen's Constitutional rights and protections ever been perpetrated by a court in the United States since *Dred Scott*? (Is the reader still refusing to face the reality that Wake County operates as a criminal enterprise as defined by RICO – Racketeer Influenced and Corrupt Organization? Read on.)

McGuire's Order violates my First Amendment right to free speech, my right to petition the government for a redress of my grievance against K, my Fourth Amendment right to be secure in my papers – court filings and protections against warrants without probable cause, my Seventh Amendment right to a trial by jury, my right to confront and cross-examine K, my right to a fair and impartial judiciary, my Fourteenth Amendment protection against a state making or enforcing any law which abridges the privileges or immunities of a citizen on the United States – deprive me of my rights without due process or deny me equal protections under the laws, and my Section 18 and 19 rights and protections guaranteed by the North Carolina Constitution.

Furthermore, Judge McGuire has no jurisdiction over my choice to represent myself and has no jurisdiction to force me to hire an attorney. (More impeachable offenses committed by McGuire.)

By his intrusion into areas over which he has no jurisdiction, McGuire incurs the charge of "Judicial trespass'"– treason – for which he must be impeached.

That said, why is my case attracting so much judicial meddling – two Wake County Superior Court Judges, two Wake County District Court judges, a Senior Resident Superior Court Judge and a Special Superior Court Judge? Why this circling of the wagons by all these judges, the Clerk's office, the Trial Court Administrators, the clerk of Court of Appeals? Who are they really defending, or for whom are these confederates conspiring to do a favor?

The answer is always the same. Ex District Court Judge and alleged sex/dug consort of K, who calls him "Rusty," -- Russell Sherrill.

Recall it was K's "Rusty" who rescued her from being caught with having filed a fraudulent assault charge. In 1984.. I show up in Court with two witnesses ready to tell "Rusty" they saw K tackle me as I tried to leave her apartment. Rusty suddenly walks out of the courtroom, without calling for a recess. When he returns, he announces, "K – Mrs. .Coleman's child has an upset stomach and there is no one else to take care of her."

Poof! "Rusty "disappears the case. Did he warn K of my witnesses? How did he know K would be home? Would he have called me if I hadn't appeared? Why didn't" Rusty play by the rules and dismiss the case due to K's non-appearance?' A judge making a personal call to one of the parties appearing before him should have been grounds for impeachment of Judge Sherrill Never happened. This is Jim Crow country. and I'm a "white nigger".

And, it was "Rusty," who signed the 1984 arrest warrant wrongly alleging I had fled to Hughesville, Pennsylvania,, where I had never been, in violation of a civil court order which did not exist. And it was "Rusty" who was allegedly seen with K at the Raleigh Foxy Lady night club. Didn't both "Rusty" and K have a history of illegal drug/pot use? Isn't an improper relationship between a litigant and a judge implied when the person appearing before him refers to the judge by his nickname "Rusty"? Isn't the evidence clear and compelling that these Wake County judges and court officials conspired as a criminal enterprise to cover-up former Judge "Rusty Sherrill's illicit relationship with K beginning in 1983?

Lest we lose sight of the fact that Shannon is the real victim of the villainy of: (1) "evil" Defendant K, (2) Defendant K's relationship with ex-Wake County District Court Judge Russell Sherrill, and(3) former and present Jim Crow Wake County Judges. Therefore, it follows that only by exposing the lies, perjury, and criminal acts of these Judge's, will Shannon become free of K's destructive control and Wake County's criminal judges.

To that end, I file a Notice of Appeal of Judge Bushfan's Order wrongly granting K's first Summary Judgment and later, McGuire's fraudulent "Gateway Orders of November 19th.

On January 4, 2015, I file a Rule 2 Motion with the North Carolina Court of Appeals inquiring as to why I have received no response from my two timely filed Notices of Appeal.

By Order dated January 6, 2015, Clerk Connell of the North Carolina Court of Appeals informs me "The motion filed in this case on the 7th of January 2015 and designated "Rule 2 Motion" is denied."

In effect, "Jane and Jim Crow" -- Judges Bushfan, Green, Eagles, Stevens, and McGuire, Clerks of Wake County District and Superior Court, Clerk Connell of the NC Court of Appeals, and sundry court officials operate as a "criminal enterprise" under R.I.C.O. – having committed the "predicate" criminal acts of fraud, perjury, suborning perjury, obstruction of justice, and aiding and abetting felonious witness tampering as defined by U.S.C. Title 18, section 1962!

Would these current Wake County judges have acted "under the color of law" with such arrogance and contempt of the Rule of Law and the US Constitution if they didn't believe Conservative judges all the way up to, and including the Conservative Scalia's/Robert's Supreme Court had their backs? No, of course not! They knew!

'…Somewhere, I come upon a case in which the US Supreme Court ruled that judges do not have immunity from prosecution for their criminal acts.

Wake County Court judges, by behaving as a criminal organization– its judges routinely committing felonious acts to support their corrupt practices – give me grounds to sue the State of North Carolina, Wake County, and its judges under the RICO – criminal enterprise statute'

Judge McGuire prohibited me from bringing any court action in North Carolina without an attorney, knowing no North Carolina attorney is going to commit political suicide by going against these judges .

But McGuire has no jurisdiction over the Federal courts, so on September 17, 2015, I sue the State of North Carolina, in the Federal District Court in Greenville, NC, its Agents, Bushfan, Green, Eagles, Stephens, McGuire, Freeman, and Connell, and in their official capacity, and Kay Silver, individually, for a finding of Fraud, Conspiracy to Commit Fraud, Violating and Conspiring, "under the color of law," to violate my First Amendment Rights to Petition the Government for a Redress of my Grievances, my Fourth Amendment Protections Against Warrants void of Probable Cause, my Fifth Amendment Protections against Deprivation of Liberty without Due Process, my Sixth Amendment right to counsel, my Seventh Amendment right to a trial by jury, and my Fourteenth Amendment right to equal protection under the laws, thereby incurring U.S.C. Title 42 Section #1983, liability, sanctions, and damages, and from multiple criminal acts as defined by18 U.S. Code #1962, 1964, R.I.C.O liability and treble damages.

Hearing nothing from the Federal Court by December 4, 2015, or 80 days since filing my Complaint, I phone the Clerk who claims to have mailed me a copy of the judge's Order dated September 23, 2015, which, I never received. (I suspect judicial hanky-panky has moved even further east from Wake County courts to the Federal Court in Greenville.

The Federal Court Judges and Clerk, operating out of Raleigh, and therefore, in at least a collegial relationship with the Wake County Defendant judges in my Complaint, also advises me, "This matter is referred to Magistrate Judge Swank for a memorandum and recommendation on the plaintiff's (me) motion to proceed *in forma pauperis* and for frivolity review."

A Motion to file *in forma pauperis* based solely on a Social Security income can be approved or disapproved in less than five minutes.

My Complaint, "the material facts which are to be construed as true and the inferences drawn therefrom viewed in a light favorable to the plaintiff, "as a matter of law, means the only reason to refer my Complaint to a Magistrate judge would be to maliciously delay – stonewall -- get rid of, or defeat my Complaint, and in so doing, invite a charge of Obstruction of Justice.

On December 7, 2015, pursuant to 28 U.S. Code #455(a) and (b) I file a Motion to Disqualify presiding Federal Judge Dever.

28 U.S. Code #455(a) states, "Any judge or magistrate judge of the United States shall disqualify himself in any proceeding in which his impartiality might reasonably be questioned, even if the circumstance is not enumerated as in § 455(b), *Liljeberg v. Health Servs. Acquisition Corp.*, 486 U.S. 847, 860 n.8 (1988).

"When the impartiality of a judge is in doubt, the appropriate remedy is to disqualify that judge from hearing further proceedings in the matter."

In a case concerning disqualification of a state supreme court justice, *Caperton v. A.T. Massey Coal Co.*, 129 S. Ct. 2252 (2009), the U.S. Supreme Court reaffirmed that litigants have a due process right to an impartial judge, and that under circumstances in which judicial bias was probable, due process required disqualification."

My reasons for my Motion to Disqualify Federal Judge Dever were (1) Judge Dever and the Defendants, all being judges working in Raleigh, North Carolina, raises the probability of collegial, social, and political association, thereby denying me due process right to an impartial adjudication of my Complaint. (2) Judge Dever, aware that a ruling against the Defendant judges for alleged criminal acts could lead to their impeachment, ("even if he were not so-aware.") *Russell v. Lane*, 890 F.2d 947 (7th Cir. 1989) -- "consequences so dire, that disqualification is appropriate regardless of the capacity (if any) in which the official is sued," *United States v. Bobo*, 323 F. Supp. 2d 1238 (N.D. Ala. 2004), increases the probability that Judge Dever would act to rescue his fellow judges from impeachment.

Seven months later, as of June 20, 2016, presiding Federal Court Judge Dever – surprise, surprise -- a Bush II appointment, displays his contempt for the Federal Rules of Civil Procedure by refusing to Answer my Motion to Recuse, thereby compounding his extra-judicious efforts to defeat my Complaint as a favor to fellow Wake County judges named as Defendants in my Complaint.

As to "frivolity review" by Magistrate Judge Swank, the "frivolity" defense is deliberately and unconstitutionally vague, subjective, and personal, and along with the Rule 12(b) (6) defense, ("failure to state a claim") a favorite "dirty trick" used by judges and magistrate judges to get rid of "nuisance" vexing, and *pro se* (representing yourself) cases.

On December 10, 2015, I file my Objection to the Court's invoking 28 U.S.C. # 636(b) (1) (12/10/15) which states in pertinent part, "Notwithstanding any provision of law to the contrary – (1) a judge **may** (Emphasis added) designate a magistrate judge to hear and determine any pretrial matter pending before the court … to dismiss for failure to state a claim upon which relief can be granted …"

The operative word is "may," presuming judgment by the judge is based on "probable cause," to wit, a legitimate reason, rather than an "automatic" referral to the magistrate as appears to obtain in the case at bar.

28 U.S.C. #636 (b)(1) makes no mention of a magistrate judge making a determination on either a motion to file *in forma pauperis,* or for a "frivolity review," meaning the judge has either misapprehended 28#636 (b)(1) and/or has cited the wrong statute.

Even granting a "frivolity review," the judge fails to cite probable cause – a reasonable justification for such a review in the face of compelling evidence that my Complaint, the material facts of which must be construed as true and the inferences drawn therefrom seen in a light favorable to the plaintiff. (me) *Harry v. Marchant*, 237, F.3d 1315, 1317, (11th Cir. 2001), thereby interdicting the judge's order for a "frivolity review," in turn, making Judge Dever liable for the charge of extra-judicial meddling to favor the defendants.

As Federal Court Judge Dever did with respect – disrespect -- to my Motion to Disqualify, Judge Dever, also maliciously fails to rule on my Motion Objecting to a "frivolity review' without "probable cause.

As of May 27, 2016, Federal Judge Dever has committed the crime of Obstruction of Justice by willfully and maliciously refusing to allow service of the Complaint and Summons on the Defendants **eight months after the Complaint was filed.**

By letter, of May 27, 2016, I request that US Attorney John Stuart Bruce, prosecute Judge Dever on eight counts of Obstruction of Justice and the US Dept of Justice to do the same.

US Attorney Bruce joins the cast of co-conspirators by refusing to respond – EVER!

The US Dept of Justice – Civil Rights Division claims "we don't handle those kinds of civil rights cases," but fails to say what kinds of civil rights cases it does handle.

Federal Rules of Civil Procedure (FRCP) Rule 72(a) stipulates that "the magistrate judge **must promptly** (emphasis added) conduct the required proceedings and when appropriate, issue a written order stating the decision."

The Magistrate's Memorandum and Recommendations is postmarked Thursday June 9, 2016, and was served on me on Monday, June 13, 2016, **nine months – 264 days after I filed on September 17, 2015. "Prompt" indeed**! (If I had untimely filed any of my pleadings, my Complaint would have been dismissed in its entirety,)

Surprise, surprise! Raleigh/Greenville District Federal Court Judge Dever rules in favor of his fellow confederate co-conspirators -- Raleigh/Wake County "Gang of Five Criminal Judges", -- by dismissing my case of documented multiple criminal acts committed by each of the Defendant Judges and my case of multiple violations of my United States Constitution rights committed by each of the Defendant judges, as being "frivolous," denying my Motion Objecting to "frivolous review, and denying my Motion to Disqualify Dever,

Now you too know the real purpose of the Magistrate Judge – Why an extra and unconstitutional hoop has been added to *pro-se* litigants to jump through – Government censorship!

Judges get to trash cases they don't want, don't like, or don't approve of, for whatever whim, bias, personal preference, or political persuasion. And lest you forget or never realized, judges have granted themselves "absolute immunity from prosecution for whatever dastardly deeds, treacherous meddling, or fraudulent injustices they commit!

"Power corrupts and absolute power corrupts absolutely" -- John Dalberg-Acton.

In *Scheuer v. Rhodes*, 416, U.S. 232, 94, S.C. 1683,1687 (1974) the US Supreme Court ruled that judges do not enjoy immunity from prosecution for criminal acts.."

I sue Judges Dever and Magistrate Swank in the Fourth Federal Circuit in Richmond Virginia, alleging (1) **Obstruction of Justice:** (18 U.S.C.1512(a) – "Use of deception or corruption or intimidation to prevent the production of my Complaint and Conspiring to Obstruct Justice--18 U.S. Code 18; #1503. (2) **Violating 28 U.S. Code #455(a)** "Any judge or magistrate judge of the United States shall disqualify himself in any proceeding in which his impartiality might reasonably be questioned." (3) **Criminal Fraud**. Judge Dever revealed his bias against me and in favor of the Defendant Wake County judges by invoking magistrate intervention for a "frivolity review" when there was *prima facie* evidence of substantial legal issues in my Complaint, "the facts of which must be construed as true and the inferences drawn therefrom viewed in a light most favorable to the plaintiff" (me), thereby contraindicating a "frivolity review." ("Justice delayed is justice denied."—Gladstone, William Penn & Martin Luther King).

I hesitate to file in the Fourth Federal Circuit in Richmond because: (1) Richmond was the capitol of the Confederacy, and likely to be even more Jim Crow than even Wake County, North Carolina. (2) At least one of the Appeals Court judges represents North Carolina. (3) Judges are a brotherhood, slightly less villainous than the Mafia, and (4) Judges take care of other judges first, lawyers from law firms according to their size and wealth, lawyers, clerks of court, court staff, litigants according to the law firm or lawyer representing them, and last, indigent and *pro se* litigants, who judges routinely punish and rule against just because they are indigent and *pro se* – "gaming the system."

As I predicted, on December 8, 2016, United States Court of Appeals For the Fourth Circuit -- case# 16-1789 (2:15-cv-00035, rules, "In accordance with the decision of this court, the judgment of the district court in affirmed."

That's it! One sentence of fifteen words to rule on my 17 page Appellant Brief comprising 18 Rules of Law and 33 cases cited in support of my Brief, and which took three weeks to research and write!

It gets worse – much worse. The record shows my Brief was submitted on November 29. 2016, and decided on December 8, 2016, or in SEVEN working days!

In the history of the United States, no court has decided a case within seven working days from the date the case was filed. NEVER! Recall Federal Magistrate Judge Swank of the Federal District Court for the District of Greenville, NC took **nine months – 264 days to ("promptly") submit her Memorandum and Recommendations!**

The Fourth Circuit Court "Affirmed by unpublished per curiam opinion."

"Unpublished" is supposed to refer to a ruling or opinion of "insufficient precedential value. However, "unpublished" can also be a way of "disappearing" a case from the public record, so that, as in the current case, no one finds out about the five conspiring corrupt and criminal Wake County judges, the Wake County Clerk of Court, the Clerk of the North Carolina Court of Appeals, corrupt and criminal Federal District Court for the District of Greenville, North Carolina, Judge Dever, and Magistrate Judge Swank's cover up of the Wake County "Felonious Five", and Fourth Circuit Judges Traxler, King, and Duncon, for their cover up of Dever and Swank -- Like I said, judges are a secret society, and like the Mafia ''operate with honor among thieves," -- they look after each other -- the law and the public's justice be damned!

"Per curiam" refers to a court's decision, ruling, or opinion by the court collectively – unanimously, often without naming the judges, and implying a routine, non-controversial, insignificant, decision.

In her Memorandum and Recommendations Federal Court Judge Swank dismisses my case against the "Felonious Five" Wake County Judges and their confederates on the meritless grounds "the plaintiff's complaint is frivolous," which Judge Swank knew, or should have known, was false, contrary to the evidence, and a fraudulent finding made for the sole corrupt purpose of aiding and abetting the Felonious Five Wake County judges – allowing them to get by with "murder"!

By signing the Order approving Magistrate Judge Swank's fraud,, Federal Judge Dever, becomes a co-conspirator of criminal Fraud.

"If you show me an appellate) judge who says he or she never lets his or her political or personal beliefs influence their decision, I will show you a judge who is either a liar or without sufficient intelligence to be on a higher bench." – John Dean. *Broken Government*, Penguin Group, NY 2007. (As can be seen herein, Mr. Dean's indictment is much more endemic than he suggests.)

The Effect of My Mother's Toxic Breast Milk on "Me"

The relevance of this back story court war -- 1982- 2018, and continuing?

Unlike Ted Williams and Johnny Carson, who married beautiful trophies hoping to fulfill the void of their mother's love, I took a direct approach by twice marrying my mother's clones, unaware, of course, of my mother's toxicity, and therefore of the danger K-posed., when, on the first night of our honeymoon, she decrees, "I've been doing cocaine for 8 years. Don't think I'm going to stop now just because I'm married," or Susan knocking on my cottage door that Friday evening, announcing, "I'm staying the weekend," then from my bedroom calling, "Come here; I have something for you."

In both instances, the "die of a toxic – fatal -- attraction – had been cast.

In K's case, (wife #2) the resulting 30 Year War Two, of psychological damage done to Shannon and me, could not have happened without being underwritten – not once but twice - by conspiring, corrupt, criminal, "Jim & Jane Crow" Wake County Judges, two Federal District Court Judges, the Fourth Circuit Judges, and a Conservative US Supreme Court.

My "mother problem" is simple: I didn't have a mother after the age of four. – not enough time, unlike Ted and Johnny, to figure out who she was – "Salvation May," who was never home as in Ted's case, or Johnny's mother, aka, the "wicked witch".

I'm forever mired in the murky memories and repressed feelings of a four year-old.

My excuse for being the most damaged – the most fucked up -- of we three -- my rationale for being among the famous Ted Williams and Johnny Carson being: (1) I had the most toxic mother-son relationship, thereby establishing a continuum for the other two, and (2) I'm the only one to explain our common chagrin

In that context, I recall being motivated by two all-consuming goals; (1) Keep my butt paddle -free lest – horror of horrors-- I get sent back to the foster home and, (2) Work my butt off to be the best -- in baseball like Ted, or Number One like Johnny, with the ultimate goal, like both Ted and Johnny, to wrench love from the many denied us by the few – our mothers.

The advantage I had over Ted and Johnny was that as a child, I didn't have to confront the ":mother problem" every hour of every day. Other than Christmas, my birthday, and Mother's Day, thoughts and memories of even what my mother looked like lost themselves in the bowels of my subconscious for the next 42 years.

The disadvantage was that my "mother problem " festered inside like a cancer erupting under the guise of chronic insecurity, a lingering sense of loss – as if someone had died, but I didn't know who – feeling alone around people – not belonging to anyone – always a stranger – odd man out – a puppy trying to get into the pet store – wanting something I knew I could never have -- having a dark secret no one must know – a basic sense of feeling unworthy …

Ted, Johnny and I had weak, feckless fathers, making our relationships with our mothers – sink or swim -- We three sank.

My father always seemed to be off to the side – to be pitied rather than respected – an example not to follow – hoping not to be like him, but fearing I might be, if not vigilant. Every mistake or failure, however slight, portended I was following in his footsteps, compounded by the fact that I was "Junior."

When his adoptive mother "adopted" me, my father and I became first, sibling rivals, and then mortal enemies. I became the weapon each used against the other. My adoptive grandmother took me under her wing – talons-- so she could shame my father by making me into the son he wasn't. My father, in turn, asserted his paternity, by taking me from her – forcing me to live with him to keep her from doing just that

I was collateral damage in their Pyrrhic war. Neither one wanted me so much as not wanting the other to have me.

By acting against my best interest in forcing me to leave Needham schools for Hollis schools, my father became my enemy, evicting me at age 15, and ordering none on my siblings to furthermore never mention my name.

My father and I didn't speak to each other from the fall of 1951 until once in 196i, but not with any degree of healed wounds when he was hospitalized with a stroke and then in a nursing home.

I did not attend his funeral in 1987, nor did Johnny attend either his mother's or father's funerals.. (My mother died in Yakima, Washington, I would have been 14. Other than my adoptive grandmother delivering me the news -- "Your mother is dead," after hanging up the phone, presumably from my mother's mother, no other discussion of my mother's death was ever made in my presence .

I was living in North Carolina when my father died in New Hampshire. My employer—the father of the autistic buy I was "tutoring" told me he would fire me if I went to New Hampshire for my father's funeral. I'm not sure I would have gone anyway.

To9 me, death's finality mutes any last words I might utter or eulogies I might compose. Funerals are for the living; the dead can't care one way or the other.

I had always pitied my father. I felt sorry his life had been so tormented. There was a time I believed my job as his first-born was to make up for his life of losses, but his losses were too many-- a mother who left him in an orphanage, a second disappointed adoptive mother who *de facto* unadopted him, his first wife left him, three children he couldn't support so he gave us up as wards of the State of Massachusetts, which placed us in two different foster homes, a biological father he never knew, the adoptive father who reluctantly adopted, him, but soon went off to France to fight World War I, coming home after the bonding period had lapsed,…If not among the living, my father created fathers from the dread – Enrico Caruso and Abraham Lincoln, the latter with whom he seemed o inherit the facial expression eternal sadness… (I did the same with Ted Williams and Thoreau.) … 40 years suffering from MS, three fingers cut off in a factory accident,, a second marriage which existed only because his second wife allowed no exceptions to her marriage vows …His losses were too daunting -- too overwhelming – too burdensome, for me to overcome, especially when I'm already weighted down by my own demons, of which he became another one..

Unworthy of my mother's love, I, like Ted, am, insecure, shy, seeking the safety of solitude , avoiding social events and parties whenever possible and feeling like a Christian at the Roman Forum for a "Save-The-Lions: rally, whenever I'm compelled to celebrate holidays, family gatherings, or high school parties..

Like Ted, I feared females, once crossing the street upon seeing three girls heading my way. `

Like Ted, I felt like a boxer in the ring with no one in my corner, no parent or surrogate I could trust to advise and support me -- left to figure out this thing called ""life" on my own, while those around me had a phalanx of family and friends advising and cheering them.

With no mother model after the age of four, thereby precluded from obtaining a working knowledge of the needs and wants of women, in turn rendering me "impossible to live with," either excluding them -- wives One and Three., or over-indulging them – wives Two and Four.

` Ted, Johnny, and I, without the unconditional love of a mother, developed dysfunctional self-destructive personalities, which repulsed the very social belonging we coveted, in turn, guaranteeing us the loneliness and sense of abandonment we so feared.

We three each had four wives. For my part, I'm subconsciously driven to find my mother. If that fails, marry her match. So, after compulsively "kissing a hundred toadesses," like a fat woman tries on shoes, I marry Wife #2 K – the worst fit of all.

Wife #4, Susan -- a perfect fit until I discover my "mommy dearest' to be a Borderline Personality Disorder as officially diagnosed in DCM II in 1972 -- two years AFTER I earned my Ph.D. in psychology! DAMN!

Patricia, Wife #1 (lasted 12 years), and like Ted's and Johnny's first wives, was the best of the bunch by far.

Nonetheless, motivated by our joint act of revenge against our mothers, each of our marriages is DOA at the window where marriage licenses are obtained.

Ted , Johnny and I, each a victim of bad parenting, became bad dads, having particularly dysfunctional relationships with a son -- Ted being exploited by his psychopathic son John Henry, who, in a perverted version of the Oedipus Complex, beheads dead Ted and freezes it. Johnny was tormented by his mental health/alcoholic son Rick, whose untimely death haunted Johnny until his own death. I was thrown under the bus by my son – rejected due to ancient grudges – his mother's abandonment of him when he was four, for which he blamed me.. .

By the time I learn that which neither Ted nor Johnny could articulate, namely a pattern among son's sucking at a toxic mother's teat – that all we three ever wanted was our mother's love -- too much damned water had passed over the dam to allow a substitute or surrogate. Ted's Louise being the exception.

Still, maybe this knowledge could at least allow me to avoid dying alone as did Ted and Johnny? Sadly no, for the search for my mother did me no better than Ted's or Johnny's attempts to replace their mother with millions of fans, hundreds of lovers and beautiful models as wives.

For it is written in the text of Time, a mother's unconditional love, once missed is lost and gone forever -- dying alone is the inevitable result of being raised on one's mother's toxic breast milk.

****